JOSEPH

OF

ARIMATHEA

JOSEPH OF ARIMATHEA

GLYN S. LEWIS

WESTHOLME
Yardley

ALSO BY THE AUTHOR

Did Jesus Come to Britain?

Daughters of Destiny

Frontispiece: Joseph of Arimathea, a cut-out, hand drawn picture discovered between the pages of a book purchased by the author from his local bookshop.

Westholme Publishing, LLC
904 Edgewood Road
Yardley, Pennsylvania 19067
Visit our Web site at www.westholmepublishing.com

ISBN: 978-1-59416-290-9
Also available as an eBook.

Printed in the United States of America.

“This author testifieth Joseph of Arimathea to be the first preacher of the word of God within our realms. Long after that, when Austin came from Rome, this our realm had bishops and priests therein, as is well known to the learned of our realm.”

—Elizabeth I, in a 1559 letter to
Roman Catholic bishops on the
precedence of the Church of England

CONTENTS

LIST OF ILLUSTRATIONS

UNNUMBERED GALLERY FOLLOWING PAGE 56

INTRODUCTION

Darkness had set in early and had covered the land that afternoon. Tremors of an earthquake, whose epicenter appeared to be beneath the city's cemetery, causing several graves to split open with rumors that some of the buried bodies had been seen walking abroad, only served to compound the growing feelings of restlessness that were troubling the city's inhabitants that day.

On a hill outside the city's walls, there stands a man. From his bearing we perceive he is a nobleman; from his garments, it is clear that he is wealthy. As he surveys the scene before him, he is waiting. He has a plan, and he knows that the time available to him will be short and that he will need to act promptly if his plan is to succeed. The scene before the man is one from which most people would shrink: three people are being put to death by the soldiers of the authority in power, using their most extreme form of punishment: crucifixion.

The two men hanging on crosses either side of the central figure are unknown to the nobleman. His interest is centered on the figure in the middle. He wants to be present at the very moment this man dies, for the plan that he has conceived is to prevent the authorities from casting this man's corpse into the smoldering pit in the valley outside the city, which is the destiny for all crucified criminals.

A shout rings out across the hillside: the man on the central cross dies. Without a minute's delay, the nobleman leaves the hill and enters the city. He goes straight to the governor's palace, requests to speak to the governor, and is granted an audience. He asks for the body of the crucified man. The governor is surprised at his request and wants to know the reason. The nobleman explains that the crucified man is his nephew, and as such he has the right to claim the body. While alive, the body of the criminal belongs to the authority; so the governor consults with the captain of the watch, who reports that the crucified man is indeed dead. The authority has no more interest in the man, and so the governor gives the nobleman permission to receive the body.

The nobleman hurries home, collects some of his servants, one of whom has obeyed his master's orders and purchased in advance a fine linen shroud in which to wrap the corpse, and together with a ladder, some tools and the linen shroud, they hasten to the site of the crucifixion. Challenged by the soldiers and some religious authorities present on the hill, the nobleman meets their challenge by showing them his authority gained from the governor. The nobleman feels a grim satisfaction as they take the mutilated and bloodied body down from the cross, for his swift action has prevented the disgrace of the body of the crucified man being slung into the common pit. The name of the nobleman is Joseph of Arimathea, and he has just taken down from the cross the body of Jesus Christ.

The name, Joseph of Arimathea, is generally well-known, either from those accounts in the New Testament Gospels that tell of his providing a tomb for the burial of the crucified Jesus, from his associations with the Holy Grail that later found greater expression in the Arthurian stories, and from the legend that has endured in parts of Britain that, as a trader in tin, copper, and lead, he brought with him to Britain the boy Jesus, as expressed poetically in William Blake's *Jerusalem* where he poses the question,

> And did those feet in ancient time
> Walk upon England's mountains green?
> And was the holy Lamb of God
> On England's pleasant pastures seen?

Joseph of Arimathea is thus not an unknown person, but he is perhaps someone of whom people know only fragments of his life and the traditions that surround him. The aim of this book is to bring these fragments together in order to provide as full as is possible a biography of Joseph of Arimathea. First, the identity of Arimathea, which through the epithet "of Arimathea" is always used to identify Joseph, is examined. The several different accounts of Joseph's entombment of Jesus that appear in each of the four Gospels are addressed in detail. We next learn of Joseph's disappearance from the Gospels, and his passage by ship to the south of France among a group of fugitives escaping persecution. We learn of Joseph's early visits to Britain as a trader in the metals of tin, copper, and lead: a journey that brings him to the area around Glastonbury for the first time. Finally, and of the greatest importance to Britain, we read the account of Joseph's journey at the head of the first mission to bring Christianity to these isles.

Above all, it is the story of a man of courage. In reverencing the body of Jesus, Joseph lost his family home in Arimathea, together with his Jerusalem dwelling and livelihood. Forced to flee Judea under the threat of Roman and Jewish persecution of the followers of Jesus, he nevertheless joined with and probably financed the escape of others who were similarly sought by the authorities. Time and again, he is revealed as a man of action. According to tradition, he appears as the head of the first Christian mission to Britain, where he lived, died, and was buried. He gave up everything to bring the story of Jesus Christ to Britain, and in return for his own rock-hewn tomb in the garden of his Jerusalem home that he gave for the body of Jesus, accepted in its place an unmarked grave in British soil. He deserves to be much better known, and the aim of my book is to give an account of the life of this man to whom we owe so much.

ONE

THE MAN FROM ARIMATHEA

Biographies of eminent persons usually begin with an account of that person's birth, the names of his or her parents, probably some details of their education, and generally cover other matters regarding their early life. In the case of Joseph of Arimathea we know nothing of these. In fact, as if to compound the mystery, no one today knows for certain exactly where Arimathea was.

The Roman historian and biblical scholar, Eusebius of Caesarea (c. 265–340 AD), together with Jerome (c. 347–420 AD), the latter best known for his translation of the Bible into Latin in the version known as the Vulgate, each wrote that Arimathea was located at Ramah (also sometimes called Ramathaim-zophim), the birthplace and subsequent home of the Old Testament prophet Samuel. The opening verse of the Old Testament First Book of Samuel says that Ramah was sited in the hill country of Ephraim. Following the exodus from Egypt of the tribes of Israel under Moses and their subsequent entering the land of Canaan where they subdued the indigenous peoples under the leadership of Joshua, the land was annexed and apportioned to each of the tribes. The tribe of Ephraim was allocated an area occupying the central and western area of the country, most of which was relatively high hill-country, and it is here that Ramah or Ramathaim-zophim—which many scholars believe later became known as Arimathea—was situated. Today the location of Arimathea is generally considered to correspond to the modern town of Rentis, about twenty miles northwest of Jerusalem, and sixteen miles east of Jaffa.

Although the place-name Arimathea appears in all four New Testament Gospels as the birthplace or home town of Joseph, apart from these four accounts there is no other record of the existence of a town or city with the name Arimathea. In Koine Greek, the spoken form of Greek which was in use when the Gospels were written, the name Arimathea was written as ‘Αριμςαθαιας, the preceding ‘ attached to the leading alpha letter indicating a breathing mark, which means that when spoken the name would have been pronounced “Harimathea.”

TIN TRADER IN CORNWALL

The question of whether Joseph of Arimathea came to Britain becomes much less improbable if we admit the possibility that he may have been a Jewish trader in those metals in which the western part of Britain abounded, and which were part of a large export trade which included countries bordering the Mediterranean.

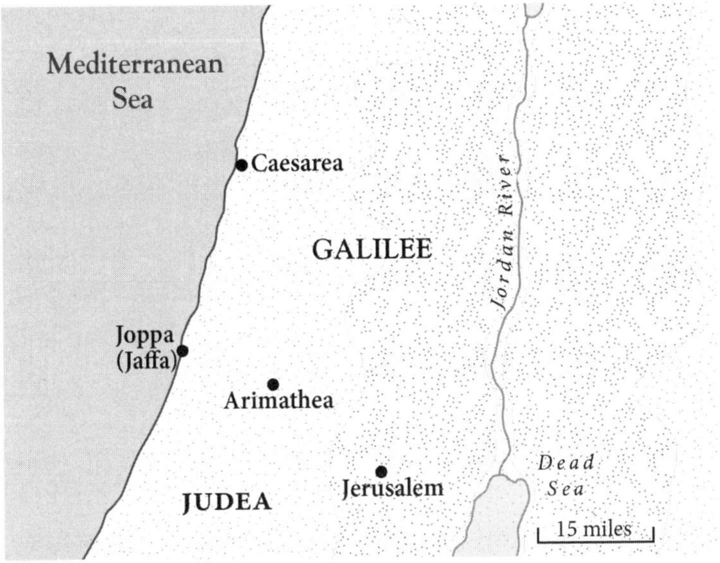

The location of Arimathea.

The Gospels as recorded by Saint Matthew, Saint Mark, and Saint Luke introduce Joseph of Arimathea as a rich man, a "much esteemed nobleman" or in the words of the Authorized Version, an "honorable counsellor," and a prominent member of the ruling council or senate. The fact that each of the four Gospel writers knows Joseph's name, provides us with some aspect of his character or position in Judean society, and that they all remembered that he came from Arimathea is worthy of our notice. There are many people who appear in the Gospel stories, some of whom play quite important roles, whose names we never learn. But each of the Gospel writers has told us the name of this man who appears for the first time in the written accounts after the crucifixion of Jesus to donate his own tomb for Jesus's burial.

In his Latin Vulgate translation of Saint Mark's Gospel, Jerome translates "honorable counsellor" as *nobilis decurio*, thus describing Joseph as a decurion. Dr. Davey Biggs in his book *Ictis and Avalon*, writes that decurions were in charge of mining districts, and it is the belief that Joseph of Arimathea acquired his wealth as a merchant trading in metals, that gave rise to the tradition that Joseph first came to Britain through being involved in the trade of transporting tin, copper, and lead from Britain to various Mediterranean ports.

The Cornish tin trade can claim great antiquity. For many centuries before the birth of Christ, various Mediterranean cultures including the Phoenicians traded with Cornwall, which at that time was the principal source of high quality tin. Biblically recorded "ships of Tarshish," operating mainly from the Phoenician port of Tyre, were the main agents in transporting this valuable metal to different parts of the world. Tin is essential for the manufacture of bronze, which in its standard form is a mixture of 95.5 percent copper, 3 percent tin and 1.5 percent zinc. All these metals are found in Cornwall, and the relative scarcity of tin compared to other metals such as copper and iron made Cornwall an important world source, with the result that there was a well-established trade with Cornwall by the fourth century BC.

Cornish tin was of the purest quality, so in order to obtain the best tin for his Roman customers, Joseph would have naturally come to Britain. Fragments of poems and miners' songs handed down through the ages make reference to Joseph and tin, and it was customary for men to chant when they worked, "Joseph was a tin man," or "Joseph was in the tin trade." The Rev. Sabine

Baring-Gould (1834–1924), novelist, hymn writer, and collector of traditional folk songs, thought this might have originated from "Saint Joseph to the tinner's aid," called out when the tin was flashed or smelted. The words of these miners' songs are now almost forgotten, but the song that began "Joseph was a tin man" possibly continued with "And the miners loved him well" as the second line, while later in the song reference was made to Joseph coming in a ship. A Cornish miners' song that has survived goes as follows:

> Here come three Josephs, three Josephs are here,
> All for to bring 'ee the Luck of the Year;
> One he did stand at the Babe's right hand,
> One was a lord in Egypt's land,
> One was a tinner and sailed the sea.
> God keep you merry, say we.

The same practice of invoking Saint Joseph's aid was also observed by some organ-builders during the process of making the sound pipes. When the molten tin was thrown onto the table on which was stretched a taut linen cloth—a delicate operation—the workman would quietly say, "Joseph was in the tin trade," at the crucial point in the operation.

It seems that Joseph was not the only Jew operating in Cornwall. Whether or not people in his pay became known as the "Jew's men," we know from Richard Carew, writing in 1602, that tin streams (for tin at the time of Joseph was obtained from surface alluvial valley gravels in a process known as streaming; mining for tin came later) were first created by the Jews using pickaxes of holm, box, and hartshorn. An example of a pick made from hartshorn can be seen today in the Royal Cornwall Museum in Truro. Later chance finds of tin were commonly known as "Jew's House tin," while Cornish folklore speaks of the "knockers" who were said to be the spirits of Cornish miners. There are names in Cornwall suggestive of Hebrew origin or, at least, of a Hebrew tradition, notably Marazion and Market Jew Street in Penzance. One still hears people speak in Cornwall of "Jews' Houses" (very ancient smelting places for tin), "Jews' Pieces" (small blocks of tin), and "Jews' Works" (ancient stream works) which were sometimes in the past called Attal Sarazin, or "the leavings of the Saracens."

Aristotle (384–322 BC), Polybius (c. 210–128 BC), and later Julius Caesar, Diodorus Siculus, Strabo, and Ptolemy all wrote about the tin industry in Cornwall. They explain the paths of transportation, overland and by sea from Britain to the various ports on the Mediterranean and elsewhere in the known world at that time. Pack animals were commonly used to carry the smelted tin overland through France in order to avoid the dangerous sea passage through the Bay of Biscay and the Pillars of Hercules (Strait of Gibraltar). Later, when we look at Joseph's return to Britain following the crucifixion and resurrection of Christ, we shall see how Joseph's knowledge of this route through France taken by pack animals enabled him to follow this same route on his journey to Britain.

FIRST VISITS TO SOMERSET AND GLASTONBURY

After visiting Cornwall to trade for tin, if he was also to collect copper and lead, Joseph's business would have required a journey to the area around the Mendip Hills in Somerset, known then as the Summerland from the fact that farming practices were only possible once winter storms and severe flooding had passed, and to Glastonbury. Copper and lead were obtained at that time from opencast mines, the remains of which are still visible, at Priddy and from other nearby sources on the Mendips.

The lowland area that lies to the north and west of Glastonbury is not like it was 2,000 years ago. The entire area was a marsh of reed-filled waters, with a few drier patches where birch and alder trees grew thickly, bounded by a vast raised bog of moss, cotton-grass, and heather. Some of the rivers in the area followed courses different from those they take today. Then, for example, the river Brue flowed sluggishly past Glastonbury Tor and turned north, not east as it does today, and drained into the river Axe.

Despite the unfavorable conditions, the area was not uninhabited. Some time around 250 BC, groups of people had made their way through the marshes that lay to the west and northwest of the Glastonbury uplands to areas where slightly drier conditions prevailed, and there they established what we have come to call lake villages. At Glastonbury there was a lake village, rediscovered in 1892, while to the west there lay a raised bog that undulated and stretched westwards towards Meare, where other smaller lake villages had been established and which were rediscovered from 1895 onwards.

It was with these lake village inhabitants that Joseph of Arimathea would have traded for copper and lead brought down from the opencast mines on the Mendips and carried to the lake villages on log boats to be traded there. Unable to bring his ships any nearer than the coast around Burnham or Uphill on the Bristol Channel, Joseph would have relied on river boats to navigate the Axe, and then on log boats operated by the lake villagers. To find a route through to the Glastonbury lake village would have required local knowledge, and Joseph probably engaged the services of someone to act as a pilot and guide him as he made his way through the waterlogged marshes. Log boats, cut from a single oak trunk, measuring in some cases over twenty feet long and capable of carrying loads weighing up to a ton, were widely used to convey goods and to travel around the area. These log boats would have been the means by which Joseph would have brought with him goods to trade with the lake villagers for metals, and then to convey his purchases of copper and lead back to his ships moored in the Bristol Channel. A preserved log boat from this period may today be seen in the Glastonbury museum.

Items found during the excavations of the Glastonbury lake village reveal that this was a busy and prosperous village and one of the richest Iron Age settlements in Britain. Harness and bridle fittings have been found, although because conditions in the lake villages would have been unsuitable for horses they were probably tethered there for short periods only. They might have been used for transporting lead from the mines at Priddy and elsewhere on the Mendips, the fine workmanship of the

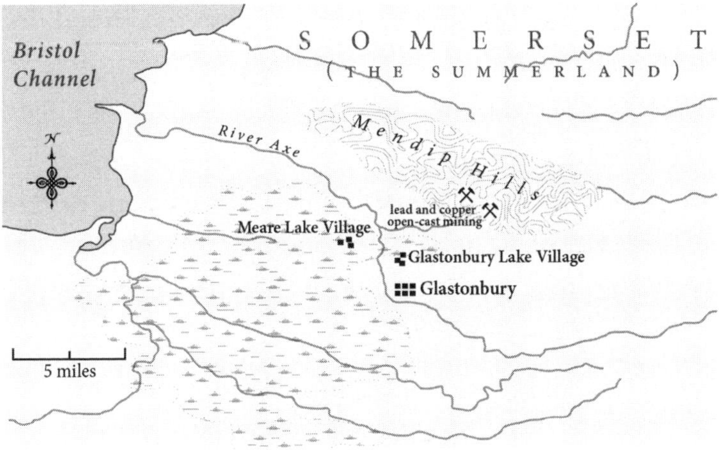

Lake villages with respect to the flooded area of Somerset, and the Mendips.

metal and bone harness fittings an indication that their owners were wealthy. Archaeological excavations have revealed that iron and bronze were both worked at Glastonbury and in the other lake villages. Iron was not smelted on-site, due to the impossibility of achieving the high temperatures required, but was traded in the form of bars that could be forged into tools. Joseph may have traded these sword-shaped "currency bars" of iron for copper and lead. Glass beads of a style suggesting that they were imported from the Continent were discovered when the Glastonbury lake village site was excavated. These, as well as amber beads from the Baltic, might have formed part of the lake villagers' trade for metals. Cordoned bowls from France have been discovered at a cave site at Wookey Hole. As we saw earlier, the trade in tin involved a journey through France from Brittany to the Mediterranean using pack animals to carry the smelted tin ingots, and bowls such as these might have been brought on the return journey to Britain for the purposes of trade.

RELATIVE OF JESUS

Associated with Joseph of Arimathea's visits to Britain to trade for metals is the legend that on one or more visits he brought the boy Jesus, as expressed in William Blake's poem, *Jerusalem*:

> And did those feet in ancient times
> Walk upon England's mountains green?
> And was the Holy Lamb of God
> On England's pleasant pastures seen?
> And did the countenance divine
> Shine forth upon our clouded hills?

Readers interested in this legend are invited to read my earlier book, *Did Jesus Come to Britain?*, which includes the work of fellow researchers, together with my own original research into whether this fascinating legend has any historical foundation. What is important to this study of the life of Joseph of Arimathea is the fact that there is an old tradition that Joseph was an uncle of the Virgin Mary, being a younger brother of her father, and therefore was Jesus's great-uncle. This will have an important bearing later on, when Joseph, in accordance with the Roman rule that only a near relative was permitted to receive the body of a crucified criminal, approaches the Roman governor of Judea, Pontius Pilate, to ask for the body of Jesus in order to give that body a decent burial.

TWO

THE BURIAL OF JESUS

Joseph of Arimathea is fleetingly mentioned once in each of the four Gospels, in each case telling the story of how Joseph buried the body of the crucified Jesus in a previously unoccupied rock-hewn tomb. There are, however, significant differences between the four accounts. This is not to suggest that some details in the accounts are invalid: witnesses to a tragedy often differ in their versions of what they saw or remembered, and at the time the crucifixion of Jesus was to many the greatest of tragedies.

Each of the Gospels records that Joseph went to Pontius Pilate, the Roman governor who had sentenced Jesus to death by crucifixion, to claim the body of Jesus. According to both Jewish and Roman law, unless the body of an executed criminal was claimed by the next of kin, the victim's corpse was cast into the smoldering pit outside the city of Jerusalem where, with other criminals who had been executed, all physical record of their lives would be obliterated. This is undoubtedly what the two high priests of the day, Caiaphas and his father-in-law, Annas, would have dearly liked to have been the outcome with regard to the disposal of Jesus's corpse.

In addition, a body had to be claimed and disposed of before sunset, which marked the beginning of the next day. If Jesus's mother had, as was the usual procedure, applied that evening to the Sanhedrin to be given her son's body in order to provide him with a decent burial, Caiaphas would almost certainly have denied her request. This high priesthood had viewed Jesus as a dangerous challenge to their authority, and the last thing they would have wanted would have been for Jesus's followers to proclaim their crucified leader as a martyr, with future multitudes flocking in pilgrimage to his tomb. But although Caiaphas and Annas could use their authority within the Sanhedrin to refuse Mary's request and dismiss her, particularly since she was a woman, Joseph of Arimathea was quite a different proposition. No doubt correctly assessing the situation, Joseph acted swiftly and used his influence to approach Pilate directly, thereby bypassing the Sanhedrin and frustrating their plans to rid themselves of Jesus completely by casting his body into the common grave outside the city walls.

It is the fact that Joseph had a right to claim Jesus's body that provides us with the evidence that he was also next of kin to Jesus. There is a tradition that Joseph of Arimathea was an uncle of Jesus's mother, Mary, being a younger brother of her father and therefore was Jesus's great-uncle. Because Jesus's earthly father, Joseph, receives little or no mention in the Gospels from the time when Jesus was twelve, most authorities are of the opinion that Jesus's mother became widowed while Jesus was still a boy. Under Roman law at that time, and possibly under Jewish law also, guardianship of a fatherless son devolved upon an uncle, and if Joseph was uncle to Jesus's mother this responsibility for the boy Jesus may have rested on him. This explains why Joseph was able to take the place of his niece, Mary, and claim the body of Jesus. The Gospels contain hints that Jesus had friends or even a relative living in Jerusalem. Catherine Emmerich, the Belgian nun who bore the stigmata and who had many visions of the life and passion of Christ, asserted that it was in the house of Joseph of Arimathea that Jesus celebrated with his disciples the Jewish Passover that Christians know as the Last Supper.

The Gospel as recorded by Saint Matthew introduces Joseph of Arimathea as a rich man who had become a disciple of Jesus, revealing that he had received at first hand some of Jesus's teaching. The Gospel recounts how Joseph wrapped the dead body of Jesus in a shroud woven from fine linen, and then placed the body in his own new tomb which he himself had hewn out of rock, probably in the garden attached to his Jerusalem property. He then sealed the door to the tomb with a large stone, and departed:

> When the evening arrived, there came from Arimathea a rich man named Joseph, who had himself also been taught by Jesus ["who himself had also become a disciple of Jesus"—Revised Authorized Version]. Going to Pilate, he asked for the body of Jesus. Then Pilate ordered the body to be given up. Joseph

> accordingly taking the corpse, wrapped it in a fine linen shroud, and placed it in his own new tomb which he had hewn out in the rock; and having rolled a large stone to the door of the tomb, he went away.

In the Gospel as recorded by Saint Mark we are told that the evening of the day on which Jesus was crucified marked the beginning of the preparations for the Sabbath. A measure of haste was thus called for, and it was essential to do something with the body of Jesus in order not to be ritually defiled and thus prevented from observing the Sabbath as a result of having handled a corpse. From Mark's record we learn that Pilate was surprised that Jesus had died so quickly, so much so that he summoned the captain of the watch to check with him that Jesus was indeed dead. Satisfied that Jesus was dead, Pilate gave leave to Joseph to receive the body. The speed with which Joseph called on Pilate to request the dead body suggests that Joseph had watched the crucifixion, and that he had been present at the moment of Jesus's death. Also, and this is of importance when we later come to consider whether Joseph was in possession of a small quantity of Jesus's blood, or possessed a shirt or garment spattered with Jesus's blood, we learn from Saint Mark's record that—probably with the assistance from friends or servants from his household, for it would have been a difficult task to perform—Joseph was instrumental in taking Jesus's mutilated and bloodied body down from the cross. Indeed, Joseph must have planned to do this since, as the following passage makes clear, he had purchased in advance a good quality shroud for the purpose of wrapping the body once it was taken down from the cross:

> And evening having now arrived, following which was the preparation, that is, the day preceding the Sabbath, Joseph of Arimathea, a much esteemed nobleman ["honorable counsellor"—Authorized Version], who himself was expecting the Kingdom of God, came and went boldly to Pilate and asked for the body of Jesus. But Pilate wondered if He were yet dead; and, summoning the captain, he inquired if He were already dead. And ascertaining it from the captain, he presented the corpse to Joseph: who, having taken it down, wrapped it in a fine linen shroud which he had bought, and placed it in a tomb which he had hewn out of a rock; and he rolled a large stone over the entrance to the tomb.

A description of Joseph as a "benevolent and just man," together with the information that he was a member of the senate and that he had not concurred with the imprisonment, trial, and handing over of Jesus to be crucified, comes from the Gospel as recorded by Saint Luke:

> And a man named Joseph, of the Judean town of Arimathea—a benevolent and just man, and a member of the senate, who had not concurred in the determination and crime of the others—who was himself also expecting the Kingdom of God, proceeded to Pilate, and asked for the body of Jesus. And taking it down, he wrapt it in linen, and placed it in a rock-hewn tomb, in which none had as yet been buried.

The word "senate" is interesting. Biblical commentators usually interpret the use here of the word "senate" as meaning Joseph was a member of the Jewish Sanhedrin that had instigated the arrest and trial of Jesus. But the senate was not Jewish: it was Roman. The Reverend H. A. Lewis, author of *Christ in Cornwall?*, believed that Joseph was almost certainly a decurion in the Roman Empire, and that, as a decurion, he would have been a member of the Roman Senate. As a Jew of high standing, it is probable that Joseph was also a member of (or possibly co-opted onto) the Jewish Sanhedrin, which would explain his presence at the trial of Jesus.

In the Gospel recorded by Saint John, we find Joseph of Arimathea teaming up with Nicodemus to embalm Jesus's body and hastily depositing it in a nearby tomb before preparations commenced for the Sabbath. Indeed, it appears that Saint John was not aware that the garden containing the tomb actually belonged to Joseph, for he reports it as simply a convenient place nearby in which to temporarily lay the body. It must be realized that this rock-hewn tomb in which the body was laid would not have been intended as Jesus's final resting-place. There would have been a family tomb somewhere, possibly at Bethlehem, but more probably at Nazareth, where Joseph, Jesus's earthly father may have been buried, and it would have been expected by all concerned that this family tomb was to be Jesus's eventual resting-place.

> After this, Joseph of Arimathea, who was a disciple of Jesus, but a secret one, owing to his dread of the Judeans, begged Pilate to be allowed to take away the body of Jesus; and Pilate granted him permission. He accordingly came and took away His body. And Nicodemus, who in the first instance came to Him by night, also came, bringing a mixture of myrrh and

aloes, weighing about a hundred pounds. They, therefore, took the body of Jesus, and wrapped it up in a winding-sheet, along with the aromatics, in accordance with the custom of the Judeans when burying. Now in proximity to the spot where He was crucified, there was a garden; and in this garden there was a new tomb, in which no one had ever been placed. There, then, the tomb being near, they deposited Jesus, on account of the preparation-day of the Judeans.

The assistance of Nicodemus in the deposition of Jesus's body in Joseph's tomb is natural enough. Nicodemus was a Pharisee, described in the third chapter of the Gospel as recorded by Saint John as "a ruler of the Jews," in the translation by Fenton Ferrar as "one of the Judean princes," and spoken of by Jesus as "the teacher of Israel." This last description comes from a story of Nicodemus visiting Jesus secretly by night who, having opened the discourse by stating that he knew Jesus was a teacher come from God, has difficulty understanding a teaching that Jesus gives during that visit. However, despite this, or perhaps because of it, on an occasion when the party of the Pharisees despatched some officers to arrest Jesus, Nicodemus attempted to take Jesus's part by stating that under Jewish law Jesus was entitled to a hearing before being convicted of a crime. Nicodemus was, however, shouted down by the other Pharisees, who argued that it was not possible that a prophet could have sprung from Galilee. The wealth available to the two men—and we have already learnt that Joseph was rich—is shown by the huge quantity of myrrh and aloes that they carried to the tomb for embalming Jesus's body: "about a hundred pounds" in weight. This measure probably refers to

Roman pounds, which if this is the case is equivalent to around seventy-two pounds in modern measurement.

So did Joseph and Nicodemus embalm Jesus's body with the myrrh and aloes? Evidence in the Gospels suggests that they did not. Darkness had set in early over the whole land at the point at which Jesus died on the cross, so there would have been very little natural light penetrating Joseph's rock tomb. We have already noted the impression of haste in order to place the body in a secure resting-place prior to the commencement of preparations for the Sabbath. The Gospel as recorded by Saint John states that they enclosed the mixture of myrrh and aloes within the winding sheet that they wrapped around Jesus's body, suggesting a hurried attempt to do something while there was yet opportunity, rather than a careful embalming of the body.

But the strongest indication that Jesus's body had not yet been properly embalmed comes from the Gospel as recorded by Saint Mark which reports that when the Sabbath was ended, at very early dawn Mary the Magdalene, Mary the mother of James, and Salome purchased aromatic spices which they carried to the tomb to embalm the body of Jesus:

> . . . he [Joseph of Arimathea] rolled a large stone over the entrance to the tomb. And Mary the Magdalene, and Mary the mother of Joses, took note of where it was placed. Now when the Sabbath was over, Mary the Magdalene, and Mary the mother of James, and Salome, bought aromatic spices, so that they might embalm him.

It is unlikely that if Joseph and Nicodemus had embalmed the body the women would have wished to embalm the body twice after such a short period of time. Further, because Mary Magdalene and Mary the mother of Joses had together seen Joseph and Nicodemus deposit Jesus's body in the tomb, they must have observed that the two men had not had the opportunity to clean and anoint the body with the mixture of aloes and myrrh they had brought with them. All the two men had been able to do was wrap the aromatics in the winding-sheet and roll the stone against the entrance to the tomb to temporarily seal it. We must concur from this that Joseph and Nicodemus's intention was to return to the tomb once the Sabbath was ended to carry out a full cleaning and embalming of Jesus's body.

EVENTS FOLLOWING THE RESURRECTION

The "disappearance" of the body from the tomb, standing as it did in the grounds of his Jerusalem property, would undoubtedly have placed Joseph in an invidious position. It is quite possible that the Jews accused Joseph of secretly removing the body of Jesus from the tomb, or of his conniving with other disciples in its removal for the purpose of giving rise to, or at the very least adding support to the growing widespread claim that Jesus had risen from the dead.

The Gospels are silent regarding how Joseph reacted to the disappearance of Jesus's body from the tomb, or even to the rapidly developing news that Jesus had risen. Certainly a lot was going on in Joseph's garden. Each of the four Gospels gives a different account: one credits an angel with rolling away the stone which Joseph and

Nicodemus had used to seal the entrance to the tomb; others speak of a young man attired in a robe of light; of two men standing nearby, clothed in robes of dazzling brightness; or of angels being seen in the tomb. John's Gospel tells how Mary Magdalene encounters the risen Jesus, but mistakes him for a gardener and asks him if he has taken the body away, imagining perhaps that the gardener had removed the body to prevent any further public interference with the garden which he probably regarded as his domain. But of Joseph of Arimathea there is no mention.

Joseph was in a difficult position. To have reverenced the body of the crucified Jesus would certainly have aroused the hostility of those Jewish leaders who had been responsible for handing Jesus over to the Romans for crucifixion. The disappearance of Jesus's body from Joseph's garden tomb undoubtedly made matters worse, and we would expect the religious authorities to have taken steps against Joseph. One account of the actions taken against Joseph appears in the *Gospel of Nicodemus*. This is an apocryphal gospel, claiming to be derived from an original Hebrew work written by Nicodemus. As the work appears to have been altered several times, its original date is uncertain. The portion relating to Joseph of Arimathea, translated from the Latin in the *Evangelica Apocrypha* (1853) by Constantin von Tischendorf, may be summarized as follows:

> The Jews, hearing that Joseph had buried the body of Jesus, sought to take him and Nicodemus and certain others. When the rest fled, Joseph and Nicodemus presented themselves, justifying their action and reproaching them for their ingratitude. They shut up

Joseph in a windowless cell, sealed the door, and set a guard. When they opened the cell, he was not there. It was presently (after the Ascension of Jesus) found that he was in his own city of Arimathea. The high priests were rejoiced at his discovery, and sent a letter of invitation by some of his friends, asking him to come in peace. On his return to Jerusalem, they asked him to explain how he had gotten away. Four angels had lifted the cell into the air, while he stood in prayer; and the Lord had appeared to him. Joseph had saluted Him as Elijah. He was told that he was not Elijah, but Jesus: and the Lord at his request took him to the sepulchre and showed him the grave-clothes. "Then I knew it was Jesus, and I worshipped Him, and said, 'Blessed is he that comes in the name of the Lord.'" Then they went together to Arimathea, and he was instructed to stay there until forty days had elapsed. The Lord then said, "I will go to my disciples," and with these words, he disappeared.

A legend concerning a far lengthier imprisonment of Joseph appears in the apocryphal *Vindicta Salvatoris*, which recounts how Joseph was imprisoned for a period of forty years, from which he was at last released by the Roman emperor, Vespasian (reigned 69–79).

Although, undoubtedly, Joseph's actions concerning the burial of Jesus would have angered those opposed to Jesus, it is difficult to imagine that they would have had sufficient grounds to imprison Joseph, let alone for such a long period. Joseph was rich, and had access to the Roman governor, Pontius Pilate. To have tried and subsequently imprisoned Joseph for forty years would have required a far more serious charge than that of giving a decent burial to a corpse, even though that corpse had belonged to Jesus who had been convicted by the high priests for the crime of blasphemy: claiming to be the Son of God.

THE DISAPPEARANCE OF JOSEPH

One of the most puzzling things concerning the Gospel accounts is that not only does Jesus's body disappear from the tomb, but so does the man who deposited the body there. He too disappears. There is no further mention of Joseph of Arimathea in the scriptures. Even the Church of England does not mention him in their list of worthies who merit being remembered: *Common Worship*, which lists services and prayers for the Church of England, ascribes no holy day on which Joseph's name is to be revered. Mary, Martha, and Lazarus, described as "Companions of Our Lord," have their day on July 29, and Mary Magdalene has a whole day to herself on July 22. But for the man who risked the wrath of the Jewish Council to rescue the body of Jesus from being cast into oblivion in a pit, arranged help and took down the body from the cross, and provided a new, unused rock-tomb for a temporary burial—nothing.

In order to break the silence on this great man's life, from this point in our study we have to allow for some conjecture, and in addition search for and examine those secular records that speak of Joseph's life from the time when scripture falls silent concerning him. The Church may have to some extent forgotten Joseph of Arimathea, but we shall discover that Britain has not.

THREE

THE FLIGHT TO FRANCE

Following the disappearance of Jesus's body from Joseph's tomb, the increasingly widespread belief that Jesus had risen from the dead, enhanced by whisperings that he had appeared to many of his disciples and had then ascended and returned to be with his father, God, in heaven, a vicious campaign of persecution, headed by the ruling priesthood and the Sanhedrin, rose against the apostles and disciples of Jesus and all followers of what had become known as "The Way."

The eighth chapter of the New Testament book, *The Acts of the Apostles*, opens with a description of the persecution against the church that was at Jerusalem, and tells how, except for the apostles, believers and disciples of the new way of living were scattered throughout the regions of Judea and Samaria. Streets were searched, house-by-house, and followers of the new way, both men and women, were dragged out and imprisoned:

> Just then a violent persecution broke out against the assembly that existed at Jerusalem; and, with the exception of the apostles, they were all scattered through the villages of Judea and Samaria. . . . Saul, however, played havoc with the church; searching house by house he dragged out both men and women and imprisoned them.

Those whom the Jewish authorities would undoubtedly have liked to lay their hands on in particular would have included Lazarus, whom Jesus raised from the dead. Indeed, Saint John in his Gospel records how the "chief priests" had earlier plotted to kill Lazarus on account of the large number of people who came to believe in Jesus after he had raised Lazarus from the dead, bringing him alive out of the tomb in which he had lain dead for three days. Others on the wanted list would probably have included Lazarus's two sisters, Mary and Martha, whose home in Bethany had been such an important place of refuge and rest for Jesus and his disciples. Women who had associated with Jesus and provided financial support to him during his ministry, including his mother, Mary, might also have been sought. It is natural to assume that these persons, who had known each other and who had been so involved with the daily life of Jesus, would have clung together for mutual help and support; and together with this group of fugitives, we must surely find Joseph of Arimathea.

Although the scriptures are silent regarding the movements or even the final whereabouts of many of these disciples and people whom the *Acts of the Apostles* says were scattered throughout Judea and Samaria, in his book, *The Drama of the Lost Disciples* (1961), George Jowett points out that we should endeavor to discover the fates of these people who had played such important roles in the life of Jesus. He writes:

> According to Acts 8:1-4, in A.D. 36, the Church of Jerusalem was scattered abroad. Even the Apostles were forced to flee. This was the year of the epochal exile when the curtain descended darkly upon the lives and doings of so many of that illustrious band. Modern Christians are chiefly familiar with the New Testament record of the favoured few—Peter, Paul, Matthew, Mark, Luke, and John—with passing reference to a few others. What became of the rest of the original twelve Apostles, the seventy whom Christ first elected, then what of the later one hundred and twenty? They are the lost disciples on whom the scriptural record is silent as the grave, particularly the two most outstanding characters, Joseph of Arimathea and Mary, the mother of Jesus. The sacred pages close upon them in that fateful year of A.D. 36, leaving not a trace or a shadow of their mysterious passage into permanent exile.

George Jowett's point is well made. Many of those who played such an important part in the life of Jesus vanish entirely from scripture following Jesus's crucifixion. Where did his mother, Mary, for instance, placed in the care of "the disciple whom Jesus loved," go? What became of Mary, Martha, and Lazarus? Similarly, Mary Magdalene and Joseph of Arimathea, who buried Jesus in the tomb in the garden of his Jerusalem home, receive no further mention. These people must have gone into hiding, for they would have been diligently sought by those who wanted to imprison them on account of their being disciples of Jesus and for having provided important assistance to Jesus during his ministry in Judea. Were they subsequently captured, or did they escape; and if they escaped, to where did they escape?

Let us consider the known facts regarding Joseph of Arimathea. It is unlikely that a man who had such great wealth, and who had shown himself to be so energetic that he had been willing to swiftly overturn the schemes of the priesthood and the Sanhedrin and provide a tomb for the crucified body of Jesus, would have sat idly by while this persecution was in progress. There is good evidence that Joseph had acquired his wealth and position through trading in metals, and as such he would have had strong connections with those living and working on the maritime seaboard. Ships arriving at and leaving from ports such as Caesarea, Tyre, and Sidon, plied their trades in different merchandise. In particular, there were vessels known as "ships of Tarshish," as we read earlier, which specialized in the trade in metals, and which regularly sailed through the Mediterranean to Spain, Gaul (France), and even as far north as Britain, where the highest-quality tin, essential for the manufacture of good quality bronze, was obtained. These ships, which in addition to goods, also carried fee-paying passengers, would have provided an excellent opportunity for Joseph and other disciples to escape by sea and flee the Judean persecution. Later, when we come to discuss where Joseph may be buried, we will examine a prophecy by the British medieval bard, Melkin, who referred to Joseph as "Joseph de marmore, ab Arimathea nomine," where "de marmore," as well as meaning "marble-like" can also mean "of the sea," perhaps clarifying for those who did not know where Arimathea was—that it was overseas—and that Joseph had arrived in Britain by sea.

In the Magdalen College Library at Oxford there is an old manuscript titled *Life of St. Mary Magdalene*, the original of which was compiled by Maurus Rabanus, archbishop of Mainz (776–856). This manuscript claims in its prologue to be "according to the accounts that our fathers have left us in their writings." Chapter 37 contains the following:

> Therefore, the chief, St. Maximus, the blessed Parmenas, the Archdeacon; Trophimus and Eutropius, bishops; and the rest of the leaders in his Christian warfare, together with the God-renowned Mary Magdalene and her sister, the blessed Martha, departed by way of the sea. Leaving the shores of Asia and favoured by an east wind, they went round about, down the Tyrrhenian Sea, between Europe and Africa, leaving the city of Rome and all the land of Italy to the right. Then, happily turning their course to the right, they came to the city of Marseilles in the Viennoise province of the Gauls, where the sea receives the river Rhône. There, having called upon God, the great King of all the world, they parted: each company going to the province where the Holy Spirit had directed them; presently preaching everywhere, "the Lord working with them, and confirming the word with signs following."

This book of Rabanus was in the catalogue of books held in the library of Glastonbury Abbey in 1148, so doubtless, William of Malmesbury, of whom we will hear more later, saw it. There are other manuscripts, but they all agree on this essential fact: that a group of people, whose number included Joseph of Arimathea, fled Judea and arrived by boat at Marseilles in the south of France. Different lists of the names of those comprising the mission exist, but they generally include the following persons:

Mary, wife of Cleopas
Martha
Mary Magdalene
Lazarus
Marcella, their maid
Trophimus
Joseph of Arimathea
Cleon
Maximin
Sidonius (Restitutus, the man born blind)
Eutropius
Martial
Saturninus
Salome
Sara, servant to Martha

A variation on the version of the journey undertaken by these refugees from the persecution taking place in Judea is given by Cardinal Baronius, Church historian and librarian to the Vatican. In the 1601 edition of his

Annales Ecclesiastice, which he reputedly spent thirty years compiling, Baronius quotes a document, the *Acts of Magdalene*, for his account of the voyage to Marseilles. Regarded as a careful historian and remembered for his dictum, *Melius silentium quam mendacium veris admixtum* ("Better silence, than a lie mixed with truth"), he states that in the year 35, Joseph of Arimathea, Lazarus, Mary, Martha, Marcella, their maid, and Maximin, a disciple who according to tradition was the rich young man in the Gospels who initially was unable to give away his wealth in order to follow Jesus, were put by the Jews into a boat without sails and without oars, and floated westward across the Mediterranean, finally landing at Marseilles.

It is virtually impossible, considering the dangerous powerful currents that flow within the Mediterranean and the sudden squalls that can arise anywhere without warning, that a boat without sails or oars could have safely made the hazardous journey from the Judean coast to the French coast. Indeed, it would not have been necessary to undertake the journey in this way. Joseph's connections and knowledge of the routes various ships followed as they plied their trade through the Mediterranean would have enabled him to arrange transport by ship to Marseilles. He doubtless carried money with him too, some perhaps from the sale of his Jerusalem property when he planned his flight from Judea. It might be that the legend that the ship made the journey all the way to Marseilles without sail or oars is not because that is how it happened, but rather that the master of the ship and his crew requested anonymity in order not to compromise future trading contracts with the Judeans through having provided their vessel for the escape and safe passage of Joseph and his fellow disciples away from Judea and those who were seeking their lives. This suggests that Caesarea was the most likely port of their departure. In his book, *St. Joseph of Arimathea at Glastonbury* (1927), the Rev. Lionel Smithett Lewis quotes a Jewish encyclopaedia, under the reference for Arles, which says that the earliest Jewish settlers at Arles came in a boat that had been deserted by its captain. (Hence the legend: "no sails, no oars.") However, the story of the voyage became so associated with the legend of Joseph of Arimathea coming to Britain that the poem *Le Saint Graal* accredited him with sailing *sans aviron, et sans gouvernal, ne ongues* ("without oar, rudder, or sails"). Today, local patisseries in Saintes Maries de la Mer sell little pastries called "navettes" (i.e., little boats): a remembrance of the arrival by sea of the little company of émigrés from Judea.

At Marseilles, Saint Maximin, La Sainte Baume, and throughout Provence one still finds the names of those first missionaries perpetuated in traditions, monuments, relics, and liturgies. Lazarus, who as we shall shortly discover, may have been accompanied by Mary, the mother of Jesus, is reputed to have become the first pastor or bishop of Marseilles. Tradition says that during the persecution of Christians by the Roman emperor, Domitian, Lazarus was cast into prison in Marseilles, and beheaded in a place which is believed to be identical with the prison which today takes his name: Saint Lazare. His body was later translated to Autun and buried in the cathedral there. But the inhabitants of Marseilles claim to be in possession of his head, which is kept in the

Abbey of St. Victor. An epitaph of the fifth century in the crypt of the Abbey of St. Victor says that a bishop named Lazarus is buried there. Some authorities, however, believe this relates to a later bishop, also named Lazarus, who was bishop of Aix from around 407 to 411, and who afterwards had passed some time in Palestine, returning later to Marseilles to end his days there.

In Vézelay, in Burgundy, relics said to be the bones of Mary Magdalene, encased in an elaborate gilt casket, are borne aloft in the town each year on July 22. There are several sites around Marseilles associated with Mary Magdalene, in particular a grotto at Saint Baume where it is said she lived as a naked hermit. Other French traditions state that Maximin went to Aix, and that Martha and Marcella went to Avignon and Arles, Martha finally settling at Tarascon where it is accepted she had a local ministry that included subduing a fierce dragon (or "tarasque"), and where she eventually died. A tenth-century Aquitaine tradition says that Martial and his father and mother, Marcellus and Elizabeth, Zacchaeus, and Joseph of Arimathea arrived at Limoges in the first century, although it states that Joseph did not remain there.

At the Council of Pisa in 1409 and again at the Council of Constance in 1417, when the abbot of Glastonbury attending these councils pressed his personal claim to international importance on the basis of Joseph of Arimathea having been at Glastonbury, the French countered the English abbot's claim with their tradition of the preaching of Mary Magdalene, Martha, and Lazarus in Provence. In more recent times, in the firm belief that these people did arrive in France, gypsies in

France have made an annual pilgrimage to Saintes Maries de la Mer at the mouth of the Rhône, where the ship bringing the Judean émigrés is said to have come ashore. The gypsies especially venerate Sara, whom legend says was Martha's black servant. The gypsies hold an annual festival in Sara's honor where, in the crypt of the Gypsy Saint Sara located beneath the old church of Les Saintes Maries de la Mer, in worship of their saint, the heat in the small chamber becomes so intense from the votive candles that it is difficult to enter the room. At the climax of the festival the gypsies carry a statue of Sara into the sea, there to receive a blessing.

Critics of these legends, such as those who dismiss the *Acts of Magdalene* as an eighth century piece of apocryphal fiction, and who in particular accuse the medieval monks of Glastonbury Abbey of inventing Joseph of Arimathea's arrival and stay at Glastonbury in order to attract pilgrims and revenue to their abbey, forget that popes and kings were already visiting Mary Magdalene's cave at Saint Baume by 500, and the cave-church of Saint Lazarus at Marseilles perhaps even earlier. Joseph was counted among their party when they landed on French soil; for those who aver that his legends are fiction, it has to be admitted that at least they were not invented in Britain.

There is evidence in the scriptures for some evangelization of France in this period, which would appear to confirm the activities of the disciples who fled Judea and arrived by boat at Marseilles. The New Testament *Epistle of the Apostle Paul to the Galatians* is not a letter to the Celtic Gauls in France, however, but a letter to the ancient Celtic kingdom of Galatia, located in the northern part of the great inner plateau of Asia Minor. A great population explosion in central Europe brought Celts into this area during the third century BC, and although never in the majority, the Galatians, gained the upper hand and ruled over the more numerous tribes of Phrygians and Cappadocians. (The word "Gaul," although it refers to ancient Celtic France and its inhabitants and is outwardly similar to the Roman *Galatia* and *Gallia*—European Celts—it is not a cognate.) Thus, when Paul uses the term "Galatia" he means either the ethnic kingdom in its geographical sense or, in its political sense, the Roman province of Galatia, which included the old ethnic territory expanded to include other parts of Asia Minor such as Lycaonia, where Paul evangelized on his first missionary journey.

However, in his second letter to Timothy (2 Timothy, Chapter 4, verse 10), Paul wrote:

> Try to come to me soon; for Demas, loving the present age, has left me, and has gone to Thessalonica; Crescens to Galatia. (Translation by Ferrar Fenton)

Here, the word "Galatia," to where Crescens has gone, is spelled in some ancient Greek manuscripts as "Gallia," meaning European Celt, i.e., Gaul, France, and some commentators interpret it as being so. If these manuscripts are the authentic record of what Paul wrote, then they undoubtedly point to participation in the evangelization of France by a companion of Paul called Crescens, whose name is Latin, and a name also occasionally found in Greek. Crescens is claimed as their founder by some churches in the Vienne and Mayence regions in northwest France, which would appear to corroborate that the word "Galatia" in Paul's second letter to Timothy means the Gaul that we today know as France, and not the province in Asia.

We know from his *Epistle to the Romans* (Chapter 15, verses 24 and 28, ". . . I have beeen longing for many years to see you, I plan to do so when I go to Spain. . . . So after I have completed this task . . . I will go to Spain and visit you on the way. ") that it was Paul's intention to travel to Spain. Whether Paul achieved this ambition is not known; but what does appear certain is that Paul would not have set out on this enterprise to the neglect of the nearer country, Gaul (i.e., France) if Gaul was not at that time being energetically evangelized. Paul, as noted above, had already written to the Galatians in Asia Minor, and it seems natural to have expected him to wish to follow this with a personal visit to the Gauls in France.

The reason that Paul felt it was not necessary to visit France is because Philip, the evangelist who had been one of the first seven deacons appointed to the Church at Jerusalem, was according to French tradition actively supporting the groups involved in the evangelization of France. The New Testament *Book of the Acts of the Apostles* (Chapter 8, verses 39, 40) says that, following the violent persecution that broke out against the Jerusalem assembly and the subsequent scattering of the disciples, Philip eventually reached the port of Caesarea, following which no more is reported of him. Caesarea is the most likely port from which Joseph of Arimathea and the other disciples departed Judea, and the reason that we hear no more concerning Philip in the New Testament might be because he also sailed from Caesarea for France.

A further indication of the number of people who were at that time spreading the Christian message in France comes from the tradition that ten (unnamed) persons were able to accompany Joseph and his son Josephes on the mission to spread the Gospel in Britain.

FROM FRANCE TO BRITAIN

There are differing accounts concerning the next stage of Joseph's life. In 1502, or shortly afterwards, a metrical poem appeared under the title *The Lyfe of Joseph of Armathia*, which contained the following passage:

> Now hear how Joseph came into Englande;
> But at that time it was called Brytayne.
> Than XV yere with our lady, as I understande.
> Joseph wayted styll to serve hyr he was fayne.
> So after hyr assumcyon, the boke telleth playne;
> With Saint Phylyp he went into France.
> Phylyp bad them go to Great Brytayn fortunate.

The poem refers here to a tradition that Joseph cared for Mary, the mother of Jesus, for fifteen years in Judea until her death, and following Mary's death went to France with Saint Philip, who then dispatched Joseph to Britain. This would make Joseph's entry into Britain sometime around 53 AD. In 1871, the London publisher, Walter William Skeat (1835–1912), edited the poem into prose form, but retained the sixteenth century spellings. Skeat's version contains additions that represent the development of the tradition that Joseph came to Britain:

> When our lorde Ihesu Criste was crucefyed, Joseph Ab Arimathia asked of Pylate the bodye of our Lorde and leyde it in a clene Sendell and put it in a Sepulcre that no man had ben buryed in, as the Euangelyst[es] testifie . . . . [Later] he became disciple to seynt Phylyp, & of hym he and his son Iosefes were baptised; and he was a messenger fro Ephese bytwyxt seynt John Euangelyst and our Ladye, and was at her departynge with other disciples; he was Constaunte precher of the worde of god as he had herde of our lorde and of our Lady, and conuertyd moche people; after, he, with his son Iosefes, went into France to seynt Phylyp and he sent Joseph and his sone with .x. others into Brytayne.

This development of the tradition was that Jesus had entrusted his disciple John to care for his mother, but that John had afterwards appointed Joseph of Arimathea to this task while John was busy at his work in Ephesus. Thus it came about that Joseph was present at Mary's death some fifteen years later, following the handover of responsibility for Mary. The tradition continues by stating that following the death of Mary, Joseph of Arimathea, together with his son, Josephes and ten others, was sent by Saint Philip to Britain.

The same order of events is told in a large manuscript known as the *Magna Tabula Glastoniæ*, which purports to tell in full the story of Joseph of Arimathea, including how Joseph cared for Mary for fifteen years until her death, following which Joseph embarked on his mission to Britain. This manuscript was in the possession of Lord William Howard, and stored as part of his collection of valuable books and manuscripts, at Naworth Castle in Cumberland. The *Magna Tabula Glastoniæ* was written on parchment affixed to six wooden surfaces attached to a folding wooden frame, probably originally designed to be affixed to a wall in such a way that it might be opened out and read as a book.

There is, however, an alternative tradition that says Joseph of Arimathea brought Mary to Britain where she died, and that she is buried in the same tomb as Joseph. For this to be true it would mean that almost all of the last fifteen years of Mary's life were spent in Britain. These two contrasting traditions each speak of Joseph coming to Britain; but if Mary did accompany Joseph to Britain it impacts on the sequence of events before Joseph came to Britain, and it sets the date of his arrival at between 37 and 38. So it is important that we examine this remarkable tradition of Mary in Britain, and how it is believed she came to be here.

To do this, we must first go back to the Gospels. The Gospel recorded by Saint John states that as Jesus hung on the cross he saw his mother standing at the foot of the cross. Beside her was the man whom the Gospel describes as "the disciple whom Jesus loved." It is probably true to say that most theologians and commentators identify this disciple as John, one of two sons of Zebedee who responded to Jesus's call to "Follow me," and who is credited as the author of the Gospel in which this passage appears.

But there is no record or evidence in the Gospels that Jesus ever called John by this epithet. Indeed, verse 2 of the final chapter of the Gospel as recorded by Saint John tells of Simon Peter organizing a fishing trip on the Lake of Galilee, in which the Zebedees—that is, John and his brother James—were present. The fishing trip was unsuccessful until they encountered Jesus on the shore of the lake, who told the disciples to cast their net on the right hand side of the boat, resulting in a large catch of fish. Verses 7 and 20 of this final chapter again mention the "disciple whom Jesus loved"; in each case it seems that an additional person—not one of the Zebedee brothers—is being referred to: possibly one of two unnamed disciples who accompanied the fishing expedition and who are referred to in verse 2. There is, however, one man who became a disciple of Jesus of whom it is recorded in the Gospels that Jesus loved, and that man is Lazarus.

Lazarus was the brother of Martha and Mary, whose home in Bethany, according to the Gospel accounts, was probably the most important refuge and place of rest where Jesus and his disciples could take a break during their wanderings and ministry. However, there came a time when Lazarus became seriously ill: so ill in fact, that his two sisters set off to seek Jesus and appeal to him to come and heal their brother. The Gospel as recorded by Saint John tells the story:

> Now a certain man was sick, named Lazarus, of Bethany, the town of Mary and Martha. (It was that Mary which anointed the Lord with ointment, and wiped his feet with her hair, whose brother Lazarus was sick.) Therefore his sisters sent unto him, saying, Lord, behold, he whom thou lovest is sick.

The phrase, "he whom thou lovest," appears once in the Gospels, and only in this passage, and it applies to Lazarus. It therefore begs the question: when the phrase, "the disciple whom Jesus loved," appears (and it is significant that it only begins to appear in the Gospel account from this time) is that disciple Lazarus? The story continues with Jesus returning to Bethany where we find that Lazarus has died. Jesus raises Lazarus from the dead, who as a result becomes such a powerful witness that many of the Jews begin to believe in Jesus: so much so that the chief priests take counsel on how they might put Lazarus to death. This would explain why Lazarus is listed among those disciples who later fled Judea and persecution, and who arrived along with others in the south of France.

Returning to the scene at the foot of the cross:

> When Jesus, therefore, saw his mother, and the disciple whom he loved, standing near, he said to his mother: "Mother, see your son!" He then said to the disciple: "See, that is your mother!" And from that hour the disciple took her to his own home.

It is to this "disciple whom Jesus loved" that Jesus entrusts his mother, Mary, and then the disciple takes Mary to his own home. We have seen that Lazarus, and not John as is commonly assumed, might be that disciple. It seems far more natural that Jesus would have entrusted Mary into the care of Lazarus and his two sisters in their safe home in Bethany, of whom he was so clearly fond, than to John and the Zebedee family with whom there is no biblical record of Jesus ever having stayed.

So when Lazarus, Joseph of Arimathea, and the others fled Judea and sailed to the south of France, it is feasible that Mary accompanied Lazarus. Mary, having been released from Lazarus's care into the care of Joseph of Arimathea who, as tradition states, looked after Mary during the last fifteen years of her life, must have accompanied

Joseph on his journey through France and onward to Britain. In his *St. Joseph of Arimathea at Glastonbury*, Rev. Lionel Lewis writes,

> I learnt from the Revd. H. A. Lewis a distinctly startling statement. Mrs. Cottrell, of Penwerris, Cornwall, an old lady, educated as a girl at a French convent in Alexandria by nuns who were members of the old French noblesse, said that she had been told by the sisters that "St. Joseph of Arimathea brought the Blessed Virgin to Britain, and that she died there." It is an amazing statement to come from modern Roman Catholics. At the most it could only mean that among the French there lingered a tradition that the Blessed Virgin had come to Britain, and that her Koimesis, or falling asleep, took place there.

In addition, Rev. Lewis raises the question, quoting E. Hutton's *Highways and Byways in Wiltshire*, "Why is England known as 'Our Lady's Dowry'?" We will return later to this matter of Mary in Britain when we reach Glastonbury Abbey where a stone, set in what was formerly the Lady Chapel, later to be known as St. Joseph's Chapel, has the words "Jesus Maria" engraved on it. If Mary did accompany Joseph and spent the last fifteen years of her life here rather than in Judea, it would set the date of Joseph's entry into Britain at some time between 37 and 38. This accords with the statement by the British monk, Gildas (c. 517–570), who wrote that "The light of Christ first shone in Britain in the last year of the reign of Tiberias Caesar," which was the year 37.

The route from Provence in France to Britain would have been familiar to Joseph. In order to avoid the dangerous sea-passage through the Bay of Biscay, the route involved shipping smelted tin from Cornwall across the Channel to the port at Morlaix in Brittany, and then using pack animals to carry the tin down through France to the port at Marseilles on the Mediterranean. Joseph, together with his son Josephes and ten other companions, and perhaps accompanied by Mary, would have traced this route in reverse, travelling north up the valley of the Rhône and then northwest towards Brittany and Morlaix, a journey taking between thirty and thirty-five days. On reaching Morlaix—where they still revere Saint Drennalus as a follower of Joseph of Arimathea—they would have boarded, as passengers, an ore-carrying ship returning across the Channel to collect another cargo of tin from one of the ports on the south coast of Cornwall favored by the Mediterranean traders. Now that they have reached Britain, we must follow Joseph and his companions as they embark on their mission to being the first to bring the Christian message to these lands.

FOUR

JOSEPH IN BRITAIN

Who were the Britons to whom Joseph came with his message of Christ, and how might his message have been initially received? No written or archaeological evidence tells of a spiritual life in Britain among the population at the time of Joseph's arrival, with the exception of the group that we call the Druids. We know from the writings of Julius Caesar on his Gallic wars that the Druids believed and taught a doctrine of atonement in which there was no other way by which reconciliation with the divine justice of the gods was possible, except through the ransoming of a man's life by the life of another man. The Christian message is also one of atonement, in which the ransom of Jesus's life brings reconciliation with God. Because of this common belief in a doctrine of atonement, Joseph's message would almost certainly have captured the interest of those Druids who heard him.

The tradition that Joseph of Arimathea was familiar with Britain through his occupation as a trader in tin, copper, and lead—metals for which traders from the Mediterranean countries had for centuries come to Britain—supports the decision to appoint Joseph as the head of the important mission of bringing the Christian gospel to that part of the world. As we noted earlier, Joseph's trade would have taken him to Cornwall for tin and to Somerset for copper and lead, and he being familiar with both these areas they would have been the natural choice for Joseph and his companions to begin their mission. There are, however, no written records of Joseph's mission in Cornwall. There are written records of Joseph in Somerset, particularly at Glastonbury, and we will examine these in the next section.

There is a Welsh tradition that Joseph evangelized large parts of Wales, where he is known by the Welsh name of Ilid, although this name also appears in a list of missionaries who came later and from Rome, in which Ilid is described as "a man of Israel." Freculphus, a ninth century bishop of Lisieux in France, says that Joseph and his party were received when they landed in Marseilles by Druids, who passed them on to the parent grove in Wales. This accords with the record of the beginning of Joseph's mission that appears in the chronicle written by John of Glastonbury in the fourteenth century. John's *Chronicle* recounts how Joseph arrived in north Wales, where he and his companions were imprisoned by the king of that region for daring to preach the gospel there. The *Chronicle* precedes this account of Joseph's imprisonment with a somewhat fabulous story, apparently copied from a book called *The Holy Grail* (which, despite its title, makes no mention of the Grail), in which 150 men and women cross the sea to Britain on Joseph's son's shirt with the purpose of accompanying Joseph on his mission, followed by a further 450 who travel in a ship that had survived from the days of King Solomon:

> There came with them (as it is read in the book which is called *The Holy Grail*) six hundred and more, both men and women, who all took a vow to abstain from matrimonial intercourse until they should have entered the land that was appointed for them. This vow all failed to keep, save one hundred and fifty; and these at the Lord's command crossed the sea on the shirt of Josephes on the night of the Lord's Resurrection, and reached land in the morning. When the rest repented, and Josephes prayed for them, a ship was sent by the Lord, which King Solomon had curiously wrought in his day to last till the times of Christ. And so they reached their fellows on the same day.

The story continues to relate that accompanying these immigrants are a certain Prince of the Medas by the name of Vacion (or Nacion) whom Joseph had baptized in a city called Saraz, along with Mordrai, a king of Saraz. Having learned of Joseph's imprisonment, Mordrai gathers together an army and goes and kills the king of north Wales, thereby releasing Joseph and his companions. No further mention is made of the men and women who crossed the sea on Josephes's shirt, nor of the ship that King Solomon had made.

Adventurous stories such as the one just related make it very difficult for the historian to assess the credibility of other parts of John of Glastonbury's *Chronicle*. But material on which you can rely with certainty from this period is in very short supply, and one has to believe that somewhere in all this there may be a kernel of truth to be discovered.

John of Glastonbury's *Chronicle* tells us that, following his release from imprisonment in north Wales, Joseph, his son Josephes, and ten others passed through Wales and a part of Britain where a king by the name of Arviragus was reigning. According to *A School History of Somerset* by Walter Raymond, published in 1906, the river Parret in Somerset marked for some time the boundary between the two Saxon kingdoms of West Wales and Wessex. If Arviragus's kingdom included part of the land of West Wales, then the territory over which he ruled would have stretched south to where Glastonbury is today. An ancient ferry crossing that has existed at Aust on the southern bank of the Severn for more than 2,000 years would have enabled Joseph and his companions to cross the estuary and continue by boat through the flooded marshes, eventually arriving at the southern part of Arviragus's kingdom. Thus, Joseph arrives at the place where he is, both in writing and by tradition, most connected— Glastonbury.

THE JOURNEY TO GLASTONBURY

There is no country other than Britain that possesses a tradition of Joseph of Arimathea arriving on a mission to spread the Christian gospel, remaining in the country until his death, and being buried there. And of all the places in Britain that claim a connection with Joseph of Arimathea, the one that makes the greatest claim is Glastonbury.

The most popularly held tradition says Joseph and his companions arrived by boat and landed at Wearyall Hill on the western side of Glastonbury. In his book, *St. Joseph of Arimathea at Glastonbury*, Rev. Lionel Smithett Lewis suggests another possible landing-place for Joseph at a site to the northeast of Glastonbury Tor. Rev. Lewis writes that huge oak trees once stood there, and that the waters must have come up to just below the oaks, from where the ancient hill-road, Paradise Lane, to the north of the Tor, leads to Wearyall Hill, joining the ancient road from Wells. A few oak trees remain there to this day, the survivors of what once might have been a Druidic grove. The oak tree was, of course, sacred to the Druids, a company of which it is believed occupied the uplands of Glastonbury and around the Tor.

In addition to using log boats to travel through the marsh and swamp, a network of tracks, some dating back to Neolithic times, criss-crossed the marshes that covered the area known today as the Somerset Levels. The best known of these tracks is the Sweet Track, which, using dendrochronology, has been found to have been constructed in 3806 BC, and is named after Ray Sweet, who discovered it while ditch clearing. Joseph and his companions might have followed one of these tracks and entered Glastonbury on foot by an ancient causeway leading to Glastonbury from the south where the town of Street now stands. This possibility accords with a tradition that Joseph founded a cell at Crewkerne, which is on a trackway that once led from Axmouth on the south coast, north to Glastonbury. It is, of course, possible that Joseph founded this cell at a later date.

JOSEPH AT GLASTONBURY

Before we examine the claim for Joseph of Arimathea settling at Glastonbury, we should recognize that there is strong opposition to it: many historians today assert that neither the historical nor the archaeological evidence supports Glastonbury's claim to being the earliest center from which Christianity was disseminated throughout Britain. Moreover, they say that the evidence for Joseph of Arimathea being at Glastonbury was invented by monks who at that time were in need of a great biblical personage, both to give them precedence when their abbot met with the abbots of monasteries in France and Spain in General Council abroad—something that was deemed worth fighting for, notably against the Spaniards who asserted priority over England by virtue of the preaching of Saint James of Compostella—and, additionally, to attract pilgrims and their money in order to restore the abbey and its fortunes, following the great fire which consumed Glastonbury Abbey on Saint Urban's day, May 25, 1184. These are criticisms we cannot ignore, and I will examine and respond to them shortly.

The principal written source for the early history of Glastonbury's claim to being the first Christian church in Britain dating from the arrival of Joseph of Arimathea comes from the writings of the monk and historian, William of Malmesbury. William of Malmesbury stayed for a time around the year 1125 with the monks of Glastonbury. Glastonbury had then an extensive library, and

William, wishing to discover the early history of the abbey and establish how old the Glastonbury church actually was, having made a careful examination of records and charters that he found in the library, wrote down his findings in a treatise titled *De Antiquitate Glastoniensis Ecclesiae*. William's manuscript is sometimes incorrectly referred to as *The Antiquity of Glastonbury*, but the aim of William's research is plainly indicated by his title for the manuscript, which correctly translates as *An Enquiry into the Antiquity of the Church of Glastonbury*. William's treatise was later incorporated into manuscripts written by two monks of Glastonbury: first, by Adam of Domerham, who brought the history of Glastonbury down to 1291 in his *History of Glastonbury*; and later by John of Glastonbury in *The Chronicle of Glastonbury*, who abbreviated the narrative of both his predecessors and carried on the history to 1342, John's work later being brought up to the end of the fifteenth century by the monk, William Wyche.

It is William of Malmesbury's treatise that some historians suggest was put together by William to flatter the vanity of the Glastonbury monks with whom he was staying at the time: an unkind charge, considering that much of William's writings contain a good deal of true history and reveal that he worked hard as a careful investigator of the distant past, in almost all cases supplying the source references for his writings. These historians aver that the monks later altered and enlarged William's manuscript for the purpose of increasing the status of Glastonbury Abbey. It is the case that the manuscript that we have today includes many details that became known and events that took place after

William's death in 1142, such as an account of the fire that burnt down the abbey in 1184, and a list of the abbots of Glastonbury down to the dissolution of the monastery in 1539. But amendments and updates to manuscripts were common and do not imply that they were always made with fraudulent intentions. This study of the life of Joseph of Arimathea has an interest in the antiquity of the Glastonbury church, particularly if it can be found that Joseph and his companions were its original founders. For this reason what especially concerns us in this matter of William of Malmesbury's original manuscript and the later amendments is where do we find the first reliable mention of Joseph of Arimathea?

An attempt to identify the original treatise that came from the hand of William of Malmesbury and separate this from the various accretions to the manuscript made down to the middle of the thirteenth century, was made by Joseph Armitage Robinson, formerly dean of Wells, who published the results of his findings in 1921 in his *Somerset Historical Essays*. Armitage Robinson clearly shows that he is well aware of the controversies over William of Malmesbury's treatise:

> It has become the fashion to throw aside William of Malmesbury's *Enquiry into the Antiquity of the Church of Glastonbury* as a careless piece of work hastily put together to flatter the vanity of the Glastonbury monks when, for some reason which remains obscure to us, the great historian had for a time taken up his abode in their house. Nothing that the credulous fathers told him was too puerile for him to record as history while he ate their bread; and when he was gone

they took his book and loaded it up with fresh fictions, so that it has no value left for serious students. This adverse judgement has seemed to be confirmed by the discovery of a tenth-century list of the English abbots of Glastonbury, which cannot be reconciled with William of Malmesbury's list in the *De Antiquitate*.

Armitage Robinson thought that William of Malmesbury had placed himself in an invidious position during his stay at Glastonbury Abbey. He also believed those portions of William's treatise regarding Arthur and Avalon, Joseph of Arimathea, and the Holy Grail all belonged to amendments made later by monks of Glastonbury Abbey:

> William of Malmesbury's *Enquiry into the Antiquity of the Church of Glastonbury* is a byword among the historians. The great Homer is found nodding: his critical instinct has been charmed into slumber by the amenities of the house which has made him welcome: moreover, his work has been falsified by succeeding generations of monks; so that what is given us under his name is on all accounts a negligible quantity. The application of the ordinary tests of criticism leads to a very different verdict. The accretions can be cleared away with tolerable certainty; and the book, reduced indeed in bulk, becomes a striking witness to the pains which its author bestowed on the investigation of the muniments of the abbey. Students of the Arthurian legend will find some of their difficulties removed by the negative results of this discussion. Arthur and Avalon, Joseph of Arimathea and the Holy Grail belong exclusively to the later recensions of the book.

There was, as Armitage Robinson points out, a "pretty rivalry" in medieval times between the great abbeys of Westminster and Glastonbury, and that on occasions spurious claims were made in this contest for historical precedence. In his opinion some of Glastonbury's claims are forgeries that were employed to finally establish Glastonbury's precedence over Westminster:

> . . . but presently she made a bolder bid for antiquity and took over the legend of Joseph of Arimathea and the Holy Grail, and so settled her date once and for all as the thirty-first year after the Passion of the Lord and the fifteenth after the Assumption of the glorious Virgin.

In order to differentiate William of Malmesbury's original text from the amendments that were made later to his manuscript, Armitage Robinson used as the basis of his study the fact that William of Malmesbury had copied selected portions of his manuscript, *An Enquiry into the Antiquity of the Church of Glastonbury*, into one of his other books, *Gesta Regum Anglorum—Acts of the Kings of the English*, in particular the third edition that William made between the years 1135 and 1140, just prior to his death. This, Armitage Robinson argues in *Somerset Historical Essays*, places a valuable instrument of criticism in our hands, which facilitates the identification of William's original version before it was enlarged and amended by the monks at Glastonbury.

Robinson found that those parts of the manuscript which William incorporated into his *Acts of the Kings of the English* make no mention of Joseph of Arimathea. For this reason, he concluded that William of Malmesbury had heard or found nothing about Joseph of Arimathea during his stay at Glastonbury, that a new chapter was prefixed to William's manuscript when he was in his grave, and that it is this additional chapter which contains the first mention of Joseph and his companions at Glastonbury.

When Thomas Hearne began in the 1720s to translate the *De Antiquitate Glastoniensis Ecclesiae* from Latin into English he found that its margins were crowded with additions to the main text, some of which were clearly in a different hand from that of the original author. The incorporation of marginal notes or even a new chapter in William of Malmesbury's original manuscript are not in themselves evidence of monks falsifying the record. It was not unusual for medieval scribes to annotate or even edit manuscripts. Some annotations even evolved into separate works. Malmesbury's *Enquiry* could have been brought up to date in the light of later findings. Manuscripts from Malmesbury, including a surviving copy of one on John Scotus Eriugena—"John the Scot," famed for his translation of the mystical works of Dionysius the Areopagite—reveal that it was William's own practice to make annotations in the margins of the writings of others.

We should also remember that the monks who were employed in the scriptorium of an abbey where all of the abbey's books and manuscripts were written or updated, were not ordinary monks: they were well-educated men, versed in the reading of and writing in Latin. Unlike our day, where desk-top publishing with its facility to insert files, and to copy, cut, and paste text enable us to edit manuscripts with ease, monks wishing to update manuscripts had either to add new chapters or place annotations in the margins. In particular, they needed to be proficient in penmanship and exercise the greatest care when handling parchment, vellum, and inks, all of which were costly to obtain. To have fabricated the story of Joseph of Arimathea and add it to William of Malmesbury's manuscript would have required collusion within the abbey and in the scriptorium, including the need to explain for what purposes the stock of the abbey's valuable writing materials had been diminished.

The manuscript of William of Malmesbury's *An Enquiry into the Antiquity of the Church of Glastonbury* is in Trinity College Library, Cambridge, in the translation made from the Latin by Thomas Hearne, published in Oxford in 1727. It is followed immediately by Hearne's *Adam of Domerham*, where the narrative is brought down to 1307. Because of its title, Thomas Hearne supposed that the whole work was that of Adam of Domerham and therefore edited the work as it lay before him in the manuscript, discriminating as best he could between the marginal notes that had been added by various people. The portion of Hearne's translation relating to Joseph of Arimathea, which Armitage Robinson believed was a new chapter written by someone other than William of Malmesbury and later prefixed to William's manuscript, reads as follows:

> Now Saint Philip, as Freculfus [Freculfus was Bishop of Lisieux in the ninth century] declares in the fourth chapter of his second book, came to the country of the Franks, and by his gracious preaching turned many to the faith and baptised them. Then, desiring that the

word of Christ should be yet further spread abroad, he chose twelve of his disciples and sent them to Britain to proclaim the word of life and preach the Incarnation of Jesus Christ, and on each of them he devoutedly laid his right hand; and over them he appointed, it is said, his dearest friend, Joseph of Arimathea who had buried the Lord. They arrived in Britain in the sixty-third year from the Incarnation of the Lord, and the fifteenth from the Assumption of the Blessed Mary, and preached the faith of Christ with all confidence. The King gave them an island on the border of his country, surrounded by woods and thickets and marshes, and called Yniswitrin. Two other kings in succession, though pagans, granted to each of them a portion of land: hence the Twelve Hides have their name to the present day. These saints were admonished by the archangel Gabriel to build a church in honour of the Blessed Virgin. They made it of twisted wattles, in the thirty-first year after the Lord's Passion and the fifteenth after the Assumption of the glorious Virgin. Since it was the first in that land, the Son of God honoured it by dedicating it to His Mother. Now that all this was so, we learn alike from the Charter of St. Patrick and from the writings of the seniors. One of these, the historian of the Britons, as we have seen at Saint Edmund's and again at Saint Augustine's the Apostle of the English, begins as follows: "There is on the boundary of western Britain a certain royal island. . . . Here the first neophites of the Catholic law among the English found by God's guidance an ancient church, built, it is said, by no human skill, but made ready for God for the salvation of men, which afterwards the Maker of the heavens . . . showed that He had consecrated to Himself and to Mary the Holy Mother of God." After the death of the first settlers the place became a lair of wild beasts, until it pleased the Blessed Virgin that her oratory should come again to the remembrance of the faithful, which happened on this wise. . . .

The chapter that follows this opening chapter tells the story of Saints Phagan and Deruvian coming from Rome to convert the Britons to the faith. It begins with the Latin words, *Tradunt bonae credulatatis annales*, which translates as "Annals of good authority record." Armitage Robinson suggests that it is this second chapter that was originally the first chapter of William of Malmesbury's whole work, saying that in his view these opening words are such as William of Malmesbury might indeed have used to begin his treatise.

Strangely, this second chapter is very like the first, telling much the same story. There are some differences: the island is called Avalon, whereas in the first chapter it is Yniswitrin; it says that twelve portions of land were granted to the earliest settlers, but they are not called the Twelve Hides; but most noticeable of all, there is no mention of Joseph of Arimathea. It is from this second chapter that William of Malmesbury copied portions into his book, *Acts of the Kings of the English*. The two do not agree word for word, either because this chapter includes changes that were made after William's death, or because William only wished to include details that were pertinent to his new book on the kings of the English.

But the important point is this: if the monks of Glastonbury Abbey *had* wanted to fabricate a story of Joseph of Arimathea arriving at and making Glastonbury the center of the first Christian mission to Britain, *this* was the chapter in which to incorporate the story: a chapter that the monks had seemingly already annotated and updated with marginal notes. To add a new chapter at the front of the manuscript, repeating more or less the same story found in the second chapter, does not necessarily point to a forgery. Rather, it has the appearance of the discovery of a piece of writing from some source that is now lost to us that was similar to the second chapter, but which had the important addition of the arrival of Joseph of Arimathea. And not possessing our editing capabilities, either William of Malmesbury or, later, the monks of Glastonbury Abbey, took the only option open to them and wrote out this newly discovered piece as a separate chapter.

CRITICISMS OF THE TRADITION

I wrote earlier that there are historians who assert that neither the historical nor the archaeological evidence supports Glastonbury's claim to being the earliest center from which Christianity was disseminated throughout Britain, and who say that the evidence for Joseph of Arimathea being at Glastonbury was invented by monks, both to gain precedence for their abbot at meetings of the General Council held abroad, and also to raise money in order to restore the abbey and its fortunes, following the great fire which consumed Glastonbury Abbey and all its treasured possessions in 1184.

With regard to the archaeological evidence, excavation of the cemetery at Glastonbury Abbey has been made more difficult by the fact that when Dunstan was

Joseph of Arimathea, from a stained glass window in St. John's Church, Glastonbury.

Joseph takes Jesus's body down from the cross, from a stained glass window in St. John's Church, Glastonbury.

Stone set in outside wall of the Lady Chapel, Glastonbury Abbey.

The Holy Glastonbury Thorn.

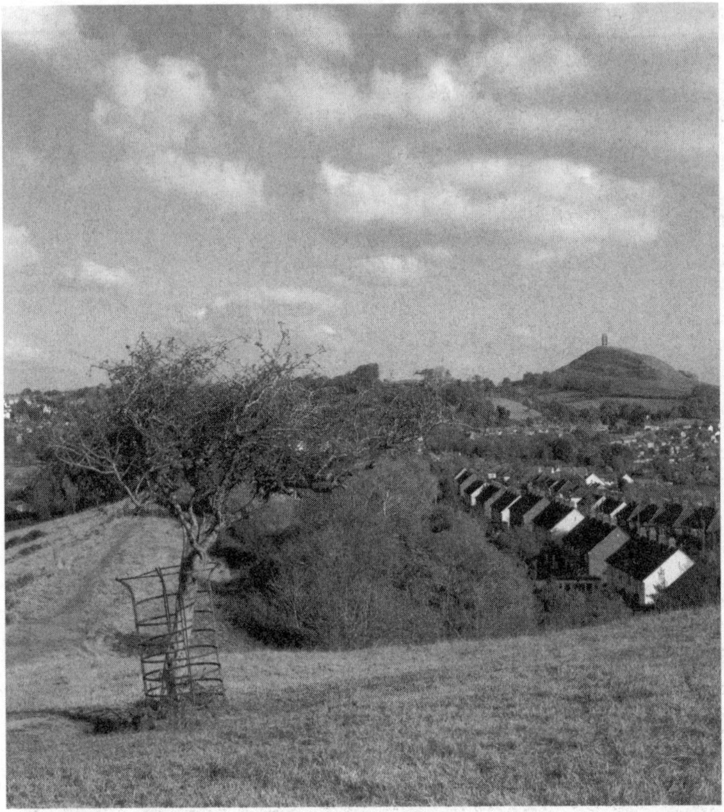

The Glastonbury Thorn on Wearyall Hill.

Joseph of Arimathea arrives in Britain, from a stained glass window in St. John's Church, Glastonbury.

Joseph of Arimathea plants his staff on Wearyall Hill, from a stained glass window in St. John's Church, Glastonbury.

St. Joseph's Chapel, Glastonbury Abbey.

The Crypt beneath St. Joseph's Chapel.

Altar tomb in the Chapel of St. Catherine, St. John's Church, Glastonbury.

Caduceus on end of altar tomb in the St. John's Church, Glastonbury.

made abbot in 940 by King Edmund I, as part of a number of extensions to the abbey he constructed a wall on the south side of the cemetery and raised the level of the ground of the original cemetery by ten feet. This raising of the ground by Dunstan explains why the monks had to dig sixteen feet down when in 1191 they were searching the cemetery for King Arthur's grave.

Excavations have been undertaken by different archaeologists, the most important of which I consider are those undertaken by Dr. C. A. Raleigh Radford who excavated in the abbey grounds between 1951 and 1964. Dr. Radford's findings led him to deduce that there is strong evidence of a Christian community living at Glastonbury in Celtic times. This community would have conducted its worship in the old wattle church, which in a restored form was still standing in William of Malmesbury's day. Digging deep in the area occupied by the earliest cemetery, which he had carefully identified as lying south of the post-1184 Lady Chapel, Radford found traces of post holes, which suggested the presence of at least four wattle oratories of a type characteristic of cemeteries that are known to date back to the Celtic period. There were indications of a small building that had been thirteen feet wide and over seventeen feet long, as well as remnants of several very early graves formed of slabs of stone set on edge and covered with a flat stone or stones laid flush with the surface of the cemetery. Two low rectangular tombs, each large enough to hold two bodies, appeared to have been for persons of special importance. Dr. Radford also uncovered the foundation of the two pyramids, described by William of Malmesbury, between which King Arthur had reportedly been buried.

Excavating in the area of Arthur's tomb, Dr. Radford did find evidence of a large hole having been dug, at the bottom of which were the remnants of other slab-lined graves, one of which appeared to be in a position of particular prominence. The suggestion that King Arthur was buried at Glastonbury highlights the change that began to take place in the sixth century, when prominent people who were not part of a religious order chose to be buried in cemeteries attached to a monastery instead of, as was formerly the case, in family burial grounds. Dr. Radford's discoveries constitute a strong argument for the presence of an early Christian sanctuary at Glastonbury.

A further criticism levelled at the Glastonbury monks who amended William of Malmesbury's manuscript is that it was done in order to gain precedence for their abbots at meetings of the General Council held abroad. Certainly at the great Church Councils of Pisa in 1409, Constance in 1417, Sienna in 1424, and at Basle in 1434, precedence was accorded to English bishops on the grounds that Joseph of Arimathea brought the Christian message to Britain "*statim post passionem Christi*"—"immediately after the passion of Christ." But these Church Councils took place almost 300 years after the death of William of Malmesbury. So the suggestion that William's manuscript was amended by monks following the fire in 1184 for the *immediate* purpose of gaining rights of precedence is difficult to substantiate. Indeed, the practice of determining precedence in Church Councils on the basis of the dates of foundation of participating churches being superior to the pope's wishes did not emerge until the fourteenth century. What is clear, however, is that by the early fifteenth century, the tradition of Joseph of Arimathea at Glastonbury had developed, probably in the main due to John of Glastonbury's writings which, as we have seen, incorporated both William of Malmesbury's and Adam of Domerham's manuscripts. From these facts we may deduce that the English bishops at the aforementioned Councils took advantage of an existing and developed tradition to assert their precedence, rather than it being the case that earlier monks fabricated the tradition in order to gain their abbots' precedence.

The belief that Joseph of Arimathea had founded the first Christian church in Britain was evidently shared by continental churchmen, since, had they felt able to challenge it, they would scarcely have been disposed to allow precedence to the English bishops at the Church Councils, where an extra representation was given to the English Church on the strength of this very claim.

Regarding the urgent need for funds to rebuild Glastonbury Abbey following the fire in 1184, it is not the idea of Joseph of Arimathea being at Glastonbury that was employed to elicit money for the rebuilding; rather, it was speculation that the famous King Arthur was buried there. According to Geoffrey of Monmouth, Arthur, mortally wounded in battle against his nephew, Mordred, had been carried to the isle of Avalon for the healing of his wounds. Clearly, if Glastonbury were found to be Avalon, the discovery of Arthur's tomb would create enormous interest and income for the abbey. In 1191, aided by the intervention of King Henry II who, according to Giraldus Cambrensis, had, when Henry was alive, told the monks that it had been disclosed to the king by Welsh bards that Arthur was indeed buried at Glastonbury, an excavation to look for Arthur's tomb was undertaken. The excitement surrounding the search and subsequent discovery of a tomb claimed to be Arthur's is shown in this account by Adam of Domerham, written one hundred years later around 1290:

> This abbot having been frequently admonished concerning the more honourable placing of the famous King Arthur—for he had rested near the Old Church between two stone pyramids, nobly engraved in former times, for six hundred and forty-eight years—on a certain day set curtains around the spot and gave orders to dig. When they had dug to an immense depth and were almost in despair, they found a wooden sarcophagus of wondrous size, enclosed on every side. When they had raised and opened it they found the king's bones, which were incredibly large, so that one shinbone reached from the ground to the middle of a tall man's leg, and even further. They found also a leaden cross, having on one side the inscription: 'Hic jacet sepultus inclitus Rex Arturius in insula Avallonia.' After this they opened the tomb of the queen who was buried with Arthur, and found a fair yellow lock of woman's hair plaited with wondrous art; but when they touched it, it crumbled away to nothing.

Again, there are historians who maintain that this discovery was a hoax, created for the purpose of attracting funds for the rebuilding of the abbey. Hoax or not, it is clear that it was the story that the tomb of King Arthur and Queen Guenevere had been discovered between the two pyramids south of the Lady Chapel in Glastonbury Abbey, and not the tradition of Joseph of Arimathea, that was employed as the means of raising money.

Indeed, until the death of King Henry in the summer of 1189, money for the rebuilding of the abbey was not lacking. Henry gave generously towards the work, and the rebuilding commenced on a magnificent scale, with a beautiful new Lady Chapel, attached to which was a vast church, parts of which were completed within a very few years. It was only when Henry's successor, Richard I, known as "Richard Cœur de Lion"—the "Lionheart," came to the throne, eager to fund his Crusade as a response to Turkish conquests of territory in the Levant and in particular the city of Jerusalem, that money from the royal house dried up. It is just at this point, when money for the rebuilding of the abbey was running low, that the timely discovery of Arthur's tomb was made. Shortly afterwards came another "windfall:" the reported discovery in Saint Michael's Chapel on the Glastonbury Tor of a charter of Saint Patrick, which the monks said had escaped the fire at the abbey through the saint having had the foresight to make and hide a duplicate on the Tor. This charter told of the life of Saint Patrick, as well as the activities of two early Christian emissaries to Britain, Saint Phagan and Saint Deruvian, who it was said came to convert Britain to the faith, and who settled at Glastonbury. In the 1920s, an Anglo-Norman translation in verse of the charter of Saint Patrick was discovered at West Pennard, where it had been used as the cover for a sixteenth century book of accounts. The following translation is taken from *A Glastonbury Fragment from West Pennard*, by Robin Flower, published in 1923 in *Somerset and Dorset Notes and Queries 17*:

> I [Patrick] was sent on a mission into a region
> that is called Ireland, a very wild land,
> by the Pope Celestine who caused me so to do
> to preach to that folk our belief.
> [Afterwards] I departed thence doing harm to none
> and returned straightway into Britain.
> I came into an isle that had to name Ynswitrin,
> so was it called of old time in the British tongue,
> in the which I found a place delectable.
> There found I several brethren well indoctrinate
> and well instructed in the Catholic faith.
> They came there after those saints
> whom saints Phagan and Deruvian had left there.
> And because I found them humble and peaceable,
> I made choice rather to be with them,
> though I should be feeble,
> than to dwell in a royal court in vigorous life.
> But because we all had one heart
> we chose to dwell together
> and to eat and drink in one house
> and in one place sleep under a rule.
> So, though I liked it not, they chose me chief
> and by fraternal force made me their guardian.

Excited by these discoveries, pilgrims flocked in great numbers to Glastonbury, bringing with them their coins in return for the blessings and remission of sins which offerings at such an important shrine promised them. And amid all this noise of King Arthur and Queen Guenevere, Saint Patrick, Saints Phagan and Deruvian, pilgrims clamoring for indulgencies and monks filling their treasury with pilgrim monies, quietly, almost unobtrusively, emerges the man who brought the Christian message and on whose shoulders rests the evangelization of Britain: the man who buried Jesus—Joseph of Arimathea.

THE DEVELOPMENT OF THE TRADITION

If the emergence of the tradition of Joseph at Glastonbury is subject to question on the basis of the credibility of the monks who annotated William of Malmesbury's manuscript, it must be remarked that history is not merely a record of how a tradition began. Compostela de Santiago has its Saint James, with an associated long-distance pilgrim route of note and international status; Karela, in southwest India has its Saint Thomas, now developed to the point where its Christian community is called by some "Thomas Christians." Each of these traditions no doubt had their tenuous beginnings; but they have developed, to the point where they are now widely accepted. Our tradition of Joseph in Britain has similarly evolved; it has been enriched by successive generations, localized especially at Glastonbury, and our study would be open to criticism if we neglected to examine how this belief grew. Perhaps the real question is how Joseph came to be linked with the tradition of an early Christian mission to Britain. Indeed, if the monks had been looking for a biblical personality to attract new pilgrims to Glastonbury, why choose Joseph of Arimathea? Why not choose one of the apostles: Matthias, for instance, whom the disciples drew lots for to select a replacement for Judas Iscariot? How is it that Joseph came to be identified as the first Christian contact with Britain? Joseph seems an odd choice, unless, of course, it is true that he came here, which is why Britain, and in particular Glastonbury, has this enduring tradition of Joseph of Arimathea.

The earliest development of the tradition of Joseph of Arimathea at Glastonbury comes, as we have seen, from amendments and additions, made probably during the thirteenth century, to William of Malmesbury's original manuscript. John of Glastonbury, writing his *Chronicle of Glastonbury* shortly after 1340, developed and even revised the earlier history of the abbey, giving for the first time a more complete account of the story of Joseph of Arimathea at Glastonbury. Included in John of Glastonbury's account are the story of Joseph's imprisonment as told in *The Gospel of Nicodemus*, the commission by Saint Philip for Joseph to lead a mission to evangelize Britain, and the receipt of a gift of land at Glastonbury by the pagan king, Arviragus. The tradition that Joseph had been ordained by Saint Philip as the head of the first Christian mission to Britain and that he and his companions had made Glastonbury the first Christian center in the land, was well established by the fourteenth century.

Shortly after John of Glastonbury finished his *Chronicle*, the abbot of Glastonbury, John Chinnock, caused a version of John's *Chronicle*, beginning with the story of Joseph of Arimathea's mission and sojourn at Glastonbury, to be produced in a large format (3 feet 8 inches high x 3 feet 6 inches wide), mounted on a folding frame. This document is known as the *Magna Tabula*, and its purpose was to be displayed in a prominent position in the Abbey Church where it could be read by visitors and pilgrims who might be encouraged by the story of Joseph of Arimathea to give generously. In addition, John Chinnock restored a small ruined chapel in the midst of the cemetery and had it rededicated to Saint Michael and Saint Joseph of Arimathea. Inside the chapel was a life-size triptych featuring Joseph, Nicodemus, and Jesus being taken down from the cross. This seems to be the earliest mention of Joseph's name in connection with a chapel.

On January 20, 1494, during the reign of Henry VII, Richard Beere was installed as abbot of Glastonbury. A Biblical scholar with a love of learning and possessing a keen intellect, Beere developed the tradition of Joseph of Arimathea at Glastonbury more than any other abbot in Glastonbury's history did. Abbot Beere established a chapel and shrine to Saint Joseph (who by now was acknowledged as a saint) in a crypt that he had had dug beneath the Lady Chapel in the abbey, and he also wrote a hymn and a collect for use on Saint Joseph's day, July 27. According to William Good, who was born in Glastonbury in 1527 and who served in the chapel as an altar boy, there was a stone image of Saint Joseph in the chapel, the fame of which became widespread and a popular place of pilgrimage, and where miracles of healing were reputed to have taken place:

> There was at Glastonbury, in a long subterranean chapel, a most famous place of pilgrimage, which was made to a stone image of the saint there, and many

> miracles were wrought at it. When I was a boy of eight, for I was born there, I have served Mass in this chapel, and I saw it destroyed in the time of Henry VIII by a very wicked man, one William Goals.

William Good records that the Feast of Saint Joseph was kept at Glastonbury for six days in the Kalends of August, Kalends being the first days of a month. The Greek Church keeps Joseph's Feast on July 31. The Church of England does not observe a feast for Joseph, who is excluded from the Church's Calendar of Principal Feasts and Holy Days as set out in *Common Worship—Services and Prayers for the Church of England*.

Abbot Richard Beere also created an Arithamean coat of arms, depicting an heraldic shield with a central cross surrounded by drops of blood, the cross flanked on either side by the two cruets which some traditions state are buried with Joseph in his grave. It was believed that these two cruets contained drops of the blood and sweat of Jesus that Joseph had collected when he took the crucified body down from the cross.

The sixteenth century saw the continued development of the story of Joseph when it was written down in a metrical poem, *Life of Joseph of Arimathea*, later edited into prose form in 1871 by the publisher, Walter Skeat. This *Life* speaks of Joseph, his son Josephes, and ten others arriving at Glastonbury, where they remained until their deaths:

> . . . after he, with his son Iosefes, went into France to seynt Phylyp and he sent Ioseph and his sone with .x. others into Brytayne & at last they came to a place then called Inswytryn, nowe called glasonburye. . . .

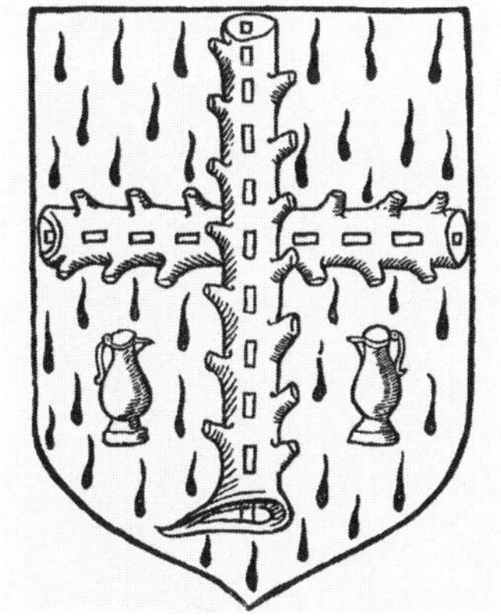

Arimathean heraldic shield devised by Abbot Beere. The coat of arms has a central cross surrounded by drops of blood, the cross flanked on either side by the two cruets believed to contain drops of the blood and sweat of Jesus.

> And after, by monycion of the Archaungell gabryell, they made a Churche or oratory of our Lady & there they lyved a blessed lyf in vigylles, fastingz & prayers. And two kynges, seynge theyr blessid lyfe, though they were paynymes, gave to eueryche of theym a hyde of lande, whiche to this day be caled the .xii. hydes and there they dyed; and Joseph was buryed nygh to the sayd oratory.

A document entitled *Visitation of Religious Houses and Hospitals*, dated 1526, contains the name of the abbot of Glastonbury, together with the names of fifty monks who were living there at that time. Although the usual practice was for monks to adopt as their surname the place of their birth or residence, examples being William of Malmesbury and Adam of Domerham, we find in this list of 1526 a new practice where monks had begun to adopt the name of a saint or hero associated with Glastonbury. Two names on this list appear to have been adopted with Joseph of Arimathea in mind: Robertus Armathie, and Willelmus Yosephe.

THE TWELVE HIDES

As we have seen, the first edition of William of Malmesbury's book, *On the Antiquity of the Church at Glastonbury*, makes no mention of Joseph of Arimathea, nor does it identify the pagan kings who gave Joseph and his companions land. John of Glastonbury revised the earlier history of the abbey, and his manuscript provides names for the pagan kings, saying that the name of the first king of the Britons to whose notice Joseph and his companions came was Arviragus. According to John of Glastonbury's account, Arviragus was not willing to accept Joseph and his companions' message of salvation through Jesus Christ; nevertheless, out of respect for their peaceable mission and because they had come from so far, Arviragus gave Joseph and his companions the island of Yniswitrin and a parcel of land on the southernmost part of Arviragus's kingdom, on which to settle and support themselves. This piece of land, which is specific to the Glastonbury area, has always been known as The Twelve Hides. A hide is an ancient British unit of land measure, the exact size of which is uncertain, but it is thought that it varied in magnitude from between 60 and 160 acres and represented a piece of land that would support one family. It is believed to come from the Old English *higid*, relating to a family or household. John of Glastonbury says that Arviragus's son, Marius, and later his grandson, Coel—he of the nursery rhyme which begins, "Old King Cole was a merry old soul," and whose only son, Lucius, is reputed to have become the first Christian king of Britain—made additional grants that caused the Twelve Hides to grow in extent, eventually covering a large area around Glastonbury. The Twelve Hides at Glastonbury are mentioned in the Domesday Book, their special significance acknowledged by recording that they were exempt from tax. They came under the strict control of the abbots of Glastonbury Abbey, and no one, no matter how important, other than the abbot could exercise his office within the Twelve Hides. When King Edward I wished to hold assizes within this area one Easter Monday, it was pointed out to him that the ancient precedence forbade him from doing so, and the king voluntarily moved the assizes outside the area covered by the Twelve Hides to a spot where the village of Street is now situated.

The grant of land to Joseph and his companions was significant because it gave them a home and the means to support themselves. Even if some of the original Twelve Hides included the marsh and wetlands surrounding the uplands, those wetlands yielded food in the form of flocks of pelicans, cranes, swans and ducks, birds' eggs and fish from the waters, as well as wild fruits such as elderberries, blackberries, and apples. These, together with wheat, barley, beans, and peas that the lake villagers had grown and harvested on the slopes of the uplands, would have provided a remarkably varied diet. The grant of land by the king also gave Joseph's company status in the eyes of the other inhabitants in the area.

But it would be a mistake if we thought that Joseph and his companions were at ease in their new settlement at Glastonbury, with twelve hides of land to call their own and food from the land to eat. They had come to Britain on a mission. It is, of course, possible that Christianity was beginning to reach Britain through Mediterranean traders arriving at England's southern shores and the Severn estuary. But Joseph and his group were the first evangelists to come to Britain with the specific purpose of spreading the Christian message. Glastonbury might have been an island, surrounded by water, fen, and marsh, but it was both an economic and cultural hub, possibly handling a lot of water-borne trade coming in by way of the mouth of the Severn. As a focal point, with well-established trackways linking it with the Midlands, Wiltshire, and the rest of Somerset, Glastonbury would have proved an ideal center for Joseph's aim to spread the Christian message to the inhabitants of Britain.

THE HOLY GLASTONBURY THORN

The tradition that Joseph and his companions arrived by boat and landed at Wearyall Hill on the western side of Glastonbury includes what has become Glastonbury's most popular legend: a thorn tree that flowers at Christmas. The legend says that Joseph fashioned himself a staff from a flowering hawthorn before he left on his journey west. On his arrival on Wearyall Hill, Joseph struck the ground with his hawthorn staff, which then grew, budded, and thereafter flowered on each Old Christmas Day, the 6th of January. The sixteenth century metrical poem, *Life of Joseph of Arimathea*, speaks of the thorn on Wearyall Hill that flowers at Christmas:

> Thre hawthornes also, that groweth in Werall
> Do burge and bere grene leaves at Christmas

As fresshe as other in May, whan the nihtyngale
Wrestes out her notes musycall as pure as glas;
Of all wodes and forestes she is the chefe chauntres.

Alfred Lord Tennyson, in his *Idylls of the King,* also mentions the Christmas-flowering thorn and its association with Joseph, and of Joseph's connection with the Grail, of which I will speak later:

This [the Grail] . . . the good saint
Arimathean Joseph, journeying brought
To Glastonbury, where the winter thorn
Blossoms at Christmas, mindful of our Lord.

The Glastonbury thorn is a Levantine species, meaning that it originated in the eastern Mediterranean, and the Arimathean legend surrounding the thorn is recognized by Kew Gardens in their literature pertaining to it. Various shoots have in the past been taken from the thorn, and there is a thorn tree in the churchyard of St. John's Church in the High Street in Glastonbury and also in the abbey grounds.

It later became the custom to send at Christmas a sprig of flowers from this tree to the reigning monarch, a fact that prompted Charles I to chide the pope because the miraculous tree contradicted the pope by blossoming on Old Christmas Day and not on the new. A mild winter can, however, occasionally bring the thorn into blossoming earlier. As I write this on Old Christmas Day in 2016, which the Anglican Church celebrates as Epiphany, the Glastonbury thorn in St. John's churchyard is in flower, and a sprig of the flowering thorn has already been sent as a gift to her majesty, Queen Elizabeth.

THE OLD CHURCH

Once settled at Glastonbury, Joseph and his companions would have required somewhere that they could gather for worship and celebrate the breaking of bread together. There are writings that point to a first century building at Glastonbury known as the "Ealde Chirche," or the Old Church. The sixteenth century metrical poem *The Lyfe of Joseph of Armathia*, later edited into prose form, says that Joseph and his companions constructed the church on the command of the Archangel Gabriel:

> . . . at last they came to a place then called Inswytryn, nowe called glastonburye . . . And after, by monycion of the Archaungell gabryell, they made a Churche or oratory of our Lady & there they lyued a blessed lyf in vigylles, fastingz, & prayers.

Buildings of the first century constructed in the style of the Britons were circular, made of clay and wattle, and thatched with reeds or heather. If Joseph and his companions constructed the building that to later generations became known as the Old Church it might originally have been circular: examples of early, circular churches are not unknown in the Levant. But Joseph's heritage and experience of the rectangular formats of the temple in Jerusalem and the synagogues in Judean towns would no doubt have had some influence on their choice of design. If instead of being circular, Joseph and his companions built their first wattle church in a rectangular format it would certainly have aroused the interest of the local inhabitants who, dwelling in their circular huts, might even have viewed the new building with amusement.

There are, however, strange references to an even earlier builder than Joseph. One such reference is contained in a letter written between 597 and 600 by Augustine of Canterbury to Pope Gregory the Great, which states:

> In the western confines of Britain there is a certain royal island of large extent, surrounded by water, abounding in all the beauties of nature and necessaries of life. In it the first neophites of Catholic law, God beforehand acquainting them, found a church constructed by no human art, but by the hands of Christ himself for the salvation of his people. The Almighty has made it manifest by many miracles and mysterious visitations that He continues to watch over it as sacred to Himself, and to Mary, the Mother of God.

The translation "by the hands of Christ himself" comes from an early copy of this letter bearing the title *Epistolæ ad Gregoniam Papam*. Augustine had arrived in Britain in 597, expecting to find the whole of the country pagan. But to his surprise he found in the western parts, into which the Britons had retreated before the Saxon invaders' advance, a British church. The island in the "western confines of Britain" to which he refers is Glastonbury, and whoever the "first neophites of Catholic law" were—whether they were Joseph of Arimathea and his companions, or the later missionaries Phagan and Deruvian sent from Rome and who it is believed visited Glastonbury around 166—they found standing there an old church that was said to have been erected by divine hands. Behind this claim is a legend, held by many in Britain to account for some of the missing years of Jesus, that he came to Britain with Joseph of Arimathea prior to the commencement of his ministry in Palestine, and during his stay had constructed a building at Glastonbury. The strange name given to the Glastonbury Old Church—"the Secret of the Lord"—appears to support this tradition. An alternative, and perhaps more likely, explanation is that it was the singularity of this building, believed as it was to be the first Christian church in England, that caused it to be kept "secret" in order to protect it from the danger of being destroyed by pagan Saxon invaders.

This name, "the Secret of the Lord," also appears in some folios of the Domesday Book, compiled in 1086, which reads as follows:

> The Domus Dei, in the great Monastery of Glastinbury, called the Secret of the Lord. This Glastinbury church possesses its own Villa XII hides of land which have never paid tax.

The name of the builder of the Old Church that appears in a manuscript referenced by William of Malmesbury is given the Latin expression, *a Deo paratam*, which translates, "by God Himself:"

> Now there was a certain royal island within the confines of the realm [of Athelstan], called in the old language of the vicinity Glastonia . . . consecrated by the gifts of God Himself. Indeed, when they came into these parts, the first neophites of the Catholic law, under the guidance of God, found a church constructed (as they say) by no human art, but actually prepared by God Himself [a Deo paratum] for the salvation of man.

Buildings constructed from wattle quickly decay and fall into ruin within a few years of their construction if they are not regularly maintained and re-thatched. William of Malmesbury actually saw the Old Church, for remarkably it was still standing in the twelfth century. Although William writes that he is unable to establish who built the church, whether it was the missionaries from Rome whom John of Glastonbury names as Phagan and Deruvian, or the actual disciples of Christ, it does appear from William's manuscript that these two missionaries discovered the church in a serious state of decay and rebuilt it. It is not recorded if they rebuilt the church using the same materials of wattles and thatch that Joseph and his companions probably used, or whether they built with wood.

When Augustine first saw the church, 430 years after Phagan and Deruvian's visit, it was again in sore need of protection from the weather. Writing in his *Acts of the Kings of the English*, William of Malmesbury records that such was the reverence Augustine accorded to "the Ealde Chirche" at Glastonbury, as it was known in Saxon times, that his companion, Paulinus, who became bishop of Rochester and later bishop of York, enclosed the church with a protective covering of wooden boards to preserve it. After this, the church was known as the "Linea Basilica," or Wooden Church, probably to distinguish it from the stone church to the east of the Old Church built by the Saxon King, Ina, in whose deed of 704 it is mentioned. This must have been the condition of the church when William of Malmesbury saw it, although now we learn that the floor of the church was paved with polished stones. In Book 1 of his *Acts of the Kings of the English*, William writes:

> The Church of which we are speaking—from its antiquity called by the Angles by way of distinction "Ealde Chirche," that is "The Old Church," of wattle work at first, savoured somewhat of heavenly sanctity even from its very foundation, and exhaled it over the whole country; claiming superior reverence though the structure was mean. Hence, here arrived whole tribes of the lower orders, thronging every path; here assembled the opulent of their pomp; and it became the crowded residence of the religious and the literary. . . . This church, then, is certainly the oldest that I am acquainted with in England, and from this circumstance derives its name. In it are preserved the mortal remains of many saints, some of whom we shall notice in our progress, nor is there any corner of the church destitute of the ashes of the holy. The very floor, inlaid with polished stone, and the sides of the altar, and even the altar itself above and beneath, are laden with the multitude of relics. . . . The antiquity and multitude of its saints have endued the place with so much sanctity that . . . [it] may be deservedly called a heavenly sanctuary on earth.

William of Malmesbury also refers to a mysterious pattern of triangles and squares on the pavement of the Old Church:

> There [in the Old Church] one can observe all over the floor stones, artfully interlaced in the forms of triangles or squares and sealed with lead; I do no harm to religion if I believe some sacred mystery is contained beneath them.

It is of everlasting regret that William did not make a drawing of those patterns on the floor of the Old Church, for they may not, as William thought, have related to something buried beneath but might instead have indicated something special about the building itself. Today, people expect a building to be functional according to the purposes for which it is to be used. In the Middle Ages, however, function was not the sole attribute required of a building. Some buildings, especially those built for worship, were designed, through number and geometry not unlike formulae found in science today, to reflect the divine and express some greater reality. The building thus became a message in stones. This was achieved by setting into the design as many of the appropriate numbers and symbols as possible so that different levels of meaning would impact on the mind of each person who entered the building.

Émile Mâle (1862–1954), who taught at the Sorbonne as the first professor of medieval art in France, wrote in his work, *The Gothic Image: Religious Art of the Thirteenth Century in France*:

> The Middle Ages had a passion for order. They organised art as they had organised dogma, secular learning, and society. The artistic representation of sacred subjects was a science governed by fixed laws which could not be broken at the dictates of individual imagination. It cannot be questioned that this *theology of art*, if one may so put it, was soon reduced to a body of doctrine, for from very early times the craftsmen are seen submitting it from one end of Europe to the other. . . . Schemes of this kind pre-supposed a reasoned belief

> in the *virtue of numbers*, and in fact the Middle Ages never doubted that numbers are endowed with some occult power. This doctrine came from the Fathers of the Church who inherited it from those Neo-Platonic schools in which the genius of Pythagoras had lived again. . . . Saint Augustine considered numbers as the thoughts of God. . . . The divine wisdom is reflected in the numbers impressed on all things. . . . The construction of the physical and moral world alike is based on eternal numbers.

The triangles and squares that William of Malmesbury observed on the floor of the Old Church might have pointed to such a reality as Émile Mâle expressed. Sadly, the engraved geometric lines were lost in the sixteenth century when Abbot Beere excavated a crypt beneath the Old Church for the worship and veneration of Saint Joseph of Arimathea.

We must remember that when the Old Church perished in the fire of 1184 (although the exact cause of the fire is unknown, it was thought at the time that it might have been started by a draught blowing a curtain or drape onto a nearby lighted candle), the loss of this, the first church ever built in Britain, was felt deeply. It was an awful catastrophe, and must have left the monks broken-hearted as well as inflicting upon them the direst discomfort. Nothing, the records tell us, was left except a bell-tower built by Abbot Henri de Blois, and a solitary chapel whose name has been lost. The ruined abbey buildings we walk around today are of subsequent date, and their ruinous state is entirely due to Henry VIII's dissolution of the abbey and the later plunder of the stones by local builders.

In 1184, shortly after the fire, we find in Adam of Domerham's *History of Glastonbury* that Ralph fitz Stephen, the son of the king's chamberlain, having been given permission by the king to spend from the abbots' revenues whatever he needed, began to rebuild a Lady Chapel dedicated to Saint Mary to correspond exactly to the site where the Old Church had stood.

There had long been a belief that the Old Church had been dedicated to Mary by Jesus himself. William of Malmesbury tells the story of how, in the latter part of the sixth century, Saint David arrived at Glastonbury from Wales, accompanied by seven bishops, to rededicate the Old Church, which had needed extensive repairs following its collapse earlier in that century. The night before the rededication ceremony, David had a dream in which he was warned not to proceed because the Lord himself had long ago dedicated the Old Church to his mother. As a sign, the Lord pierced David's hand, a wound which miraculously healed itself during the consecration of the Mass the following day. Hence, the chapel that Ralph fitz Stephen built on the site of the Old Church became the Lady Chapel, dedicated to Mary. The rebuilding of the Lady Chapel was completed in two years and consecrated by Reginald fitz Jocelin, bishop of Bath, on June 11, 1186.

Following the dissolution of all monasteries at the command of Henry VIII in 1539, the Lady Chapel along with the other abbey buildings was destroyed. The abbey quickly became a ruin; many of the stones were taken away and reused in buildings in the town; others were used in the construction of a new causeway road to Wells. Some archaeological surveys and excavations were carried out in the nineteenth century, most notably by Professor Robert Willis, who published his *Architectural History of Glastonbury Abbey* in 1866. But in the first years of the twentieth century, the Church of England bought the abbey ruins at auction and fresh excavations began. It was Frederick Bligh Bond, who was appointed director of excavations at Glastonbury in 1908 and diocesan architect in 1909, who first established the layout and size of the Lady Chapel that had been built on the site of the Old Church. Although Bligh Bond parted company with the abbey trustees over conflicting views concerning an apsidal end to the Edgar Chapel at the east end of the Abbey Church and his methods of enquiry into the location of the foundations of the abbey through supposed contact with discarnate spirits of former monks, his discovery of the site, walls and, measurements of the Lady Chapel were accepted and never questioned.

Bligh Bond believed that the church that Joseph of Arimathea originally built was circular, with Joseph and his companions dwelling in circular huts after the style of the Britons around the church, and that it was later, possibly when the missionaries Phagan and Deruvian restored the church, that the church became rectangular in shape. He also discovered remains of a stone wall to the north of the church, which he believed dated from the time when Herlewin was abbot of Glastonbury between A.D. 1101 and 1120. The following figure shows Bligh Bond's drawing of the chapel's development.

Two hundred years after Ralph fitz Stephen built his chapel on the site of the Old Church, a brass plate was mounted on a pillar erected to the north of the chapel.

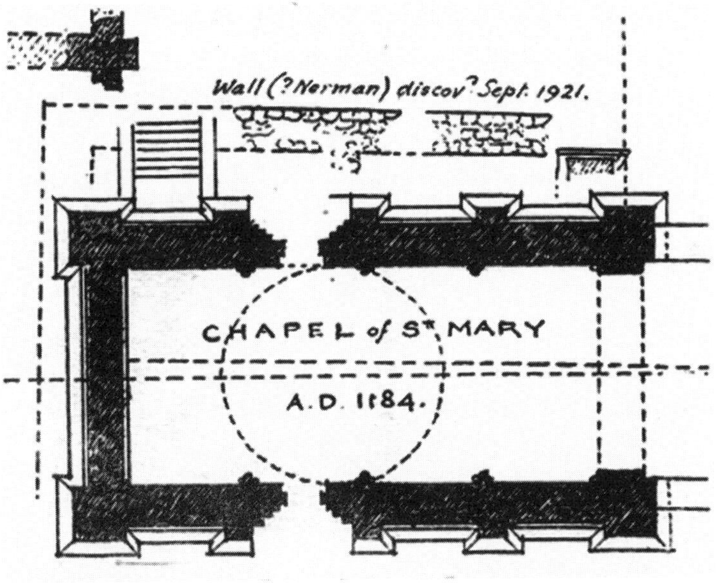

Frederick Bligh Bond's drawing of the development of the Old Church from a circular design to the rectangular form when the Lady Chapel was rebuilt following the great fire in 1184. Note the alignment of the rectangular chapel being 3 degrees north of the east-west axis.

The purpose of this was stated as follows:

> Lest the site or size of the earlier church should come to be forgotten . . . its length was 60 feet westward . . . its width 26 feet.

This brass plate is now apparently lost, and we have to rely on a representation of it in a work called *Concilia*, dating from 1639. It is not known who erected the brass plate and pillar, or from what memory or writings caused them to state that the width and length of the Old Church had been 26 feet by 60 feet. These measurements are different from those of Ralph fitz Stephen's chapel as excavated by Bligh Bond.

The argument that Ralph fitz Stephen built his chapel on the precise site and followed the exact dimensions of the Old Church is strengthened by the fact that his chapel does not point precisely east. The chapel deviates at its eastern end approximately 3 degrees north of the east-west axis that the remainder of the great abbey church follows. Ralph fitz Stephen had the opportunity to build and align his chapel to follow the normal east-west axis, and the fact that he did not straighten the axis suggests that he was faithfully following the design of the Old Church as it had been prior to the fire.

Using the standard British foot of twelve inches as his unit of measurement, which Frederick Bligh Bond believed Ralph fitz Stephen would have used when building his chapel, the British foot by then having largely superseded the earlier Romano-British foot of approximately 11.5 inches, Bligh Bond's excavations found that the width of Ralph fitz Stephen's chapel as measured between the outer faces of the central buttresses was 37 feet, and the length close to 64 feet.

As expressed by Émile Mâle, quoted earlier in this section on the Old Church with regard to the belief held by craftsmen of the Middle Ages in the virtue and power of numbers, Bligh Bond believed that these dimensions of Ralph fitz Stephen's chapel were significant. Frederick Bligh Bond had, together with the Rev. Thomas Simcox Lea, vicar of St. Austell in Cornwall, earlier made and published a study of gematria, a method of spelling out a word or group of words according to the numerical value of the letters, in accordance with a set system. The use of letters to signify numbers, or numbers to signify letters, is ancient and was known both to the Babylonians and to the Greeks. The first recorded use of it is on an inscription of Sargon II (727–707 BC) which says that the king built a famous wall 16,283 cubits in length to correspond with the numerical value of his name.

There are two ways of counting in gematria, each based on tables known as Canons: there is a Lesser Canon, when the Hebrew alphabet is being used, and a Greater Canon when Greek is used. In his book, *The Gate of Remembrance*, Bligh Bond relates how he took the name, Jesus Christ, which in Greek reads **ΙΗΣΟΥΣ ΧΡΙΣΤΟΣ**, and applied the values for these letters from the Greater Canon to arrive at the following numbers and totals:

I = 10, **H** = 8, **Σ** = 200, **O** = 70, **Y** = 400, **Σ** = 200,
Total = 888
X = 600, **P** = 100, **I** = 10, **Σ** = 200, **T** = 300, **O** = 70,
Σ = 200, Total = 1480
These two totals, 888 and 1480, can be expressed as:
888 = 37 x 24, and 1480 = 37 x 40

Bligh Bond believed he had found, using the rules of gematria, that the values attached to the name Jesus Christ, written in the Greek of the New Testament Gospels, corresponded exactly to the measurements of Ralph fitz Stephen's Lady Chapel. According to Bligh Bond, Ralph fitz Stephen had built his chapel 37 feet wide, while the sum of 24 and 40 shown in Bligh Bond's calculation equals the length of Ralph fitz Stephen's chapel: 64 feet. The area of the chapel was thus 37 x 64, which is 2368 feet, which when halved is 1184, which is both the date of the fire and also the date the chapel was rebuilt.

Today, when we stand in the ruins of this Lady Chapel in Glastonbury Abbey, now renamed St. Joseph's Chapel, on the site of the first Christian church in Britain which would have been the church in which Joseph of Arimathea and his companions met for worship and the breaking of bread together, and which was lovingly maintained and restored for over eleven hundred years, there is the thought that the chapel might, following its restoration in 1184, have included an architectural embodiment of the Greek name for Jesus Christ.

We have come a very long way in time from Joseph's church, and it is impossible to say how the restored Lady Chapel related in shape and size to Joseph's original church. Also, not everyone will agree with Frederick Bligh Bond's thesis. Perhaps we can do no better than to quote again William of Malmesbury's words concerning the chapel:

> I do no harm to religion if I believe some sacred mystery is contained beneath them.

THE GRAIL

Representations of Joseph of Arimathea in stained glass and other iconography usually depict Joseph holding two cruets in which it was said he had collected the blood and sweat of Jesus when Joseph took Jesus's body down from the cross. There is a strong connection between these depictions of Joseph and the legend of the Grail (sometimes spelled Graal).

It was a late development in the history of the Grail, mainly through French Grail romances, that caused the subject to become associated with Joseph of Arimathea. The origins and variations of this fascinating subject are many indeed. The Grail has connections, often contradictory, to ancient cults and religions, to myth, and in particular to the Arthurian legends, all seeming to defy attempts of a single interpretation, whether Celtic or Christian. In her book, *From Ritual to Romance: The Search for the Grail*, Jessie L. Weston explores the legend's earliest roots, tracing the origins of the Grail saga back to ancient vegetation rituals whose purpose was to encourage better harvests: rituals that developed over a long period of time until the Celts and Christians embellished the story.

When the Grail first appears in Celtic stories, it is described as a marvellous vessel that feeds those who partake from it without the vessel becoming exhausted of its contents, or else the vessel miraculously revives or heals the person. By the fifteenth century the image of the Grail had become an apparition of the cup out of which Jesus and his disciples drank from at the Last Supper. This cup or chalice, radiant with light, wrought of the purest gold and inlaid with incomparable precious stones, sometimes appeared at the hands of an angel, while at other times it seemed to move of its own accord. A vision of the Grail was not granted to everyone: in the Arthurian stories, for example, the experience of seeing the Grail was reserved for knights who had kept themselves chaste. The Grail became connected with Joseph of Arimathea when it developed into a story of how Joseph took the cup that was used at the Last Supper and used it to catch drops of Jesus's blood when Jesus's body was being taken down from the cross.

A story of how the cup used at the Last Supper came into Joseph's possession appears in *Mystic Gleams from the Holy Grail* by Dr. Francis Rolt-Wheeler. Titled, *The Story of Obed*, it tells how the disciples (named Peter and John, in Luke's Gospel) are instructed by Jesus to look out for and follow a man carrying a pitcher of water, who will lead them to the house of Obed where Jesus and his disciples are to celebrate the Passover meal that later becomes known as the Last Supper. Obed, an old man, tells the disciples how a bodiless hand had set a richly jewelled cup on his table in preparation for the supper. Later, after the supper was ended, Judas returns to steal the cup; but as his hand touches it he suddenly realizes the baseness of his betrayal, and he is seized with despair. Wild-eyed and dishevelled, he thrusts the cup into the hand of Simon the Leper, telling him to take the cup to the Roman governor, Pontius Pilate. The cup affects Pilate in the same way, and when Joseph of Arimathea comes to beg the body of Jesus, the distracted Roman implores him to take the cup away. As Joseph holds the cup, he receives a vision of himself bearing it to far-off lands. The cup also appears luminously to Obed as he lies dying.

Although Dr. Rolt-Wheeler provides no reference for the source of his story, the part that tells of the cup being passed from Simon the Leper to Pontius Pilate appears in the poem *Joseph d'Arimathie* by Robert de Boron.

Joseph d'Arimathie is a five-part sequence of poems written by Robert de Boron in around 1200 that first connects Joseph of Arimathea with the Grail. In de Boron's poem, also known as *Le Roman de l'estoire dou*

Graal, we learn that during their wanderings, certain of Joseph's companions fell into sin. Joseph, together with his companions, his brother-in-law, Bron, and the latter's twelve sons, then set sail for the "land to the west." On the journey, the occupants of the boat become famished for lack of food. For some unexplained reason, Joseph is unaware of the crisis until Bron informs him of it. Joseph prays for aid and counsel from the Grail, and a voice is heard from heaven commanding Bron to catch a fish. Joseph prepares a table with the Grail, covered with a cloth, placed in the center opposite his own seat, and the large fish that Bron has caught placed on the other side. This fish in the presence of the Grail provides a mystic meal from which the unworthy cannot partake; thus those who had sinned were separated from the righteous, who are rescued from starvation through feeding daily on the fish.

A later French prose romance, *Perlesvaus*, relates how Joseph collected Jesus's blood, and was later imprisoned for burying Jesus in the tomb that Joseph had prepared for his own use. Miraculously escaping from prison, Joseph comes to Britain, where he becomes the ancestor of each of King Arthur's Knights of the Round Table. Joseph's niece, Iglais, gives birth to Perlesvaus, who achieves the coveted vision of the Grail. The story then tells how Joseph places in a castle called Perilous the linen shroud in which the body of Jesus had been wrapped, and that after his death Joseph is buried outside the Grail castle. When Perlesvaus departs from the Grail castle he takes Joseph's body with him, which is then carried on a ship to the Other World. At the end of *Perlesvaus* the author tells us that:

> The Latin from whence this history was drawn into Romance was taken in the Isle of Avalon, in a holy house of religion that standeth at the head of the Moors Adventurous, there where King Arthur and Queen Guenievere lie, according to the witness of good men religious that are therein, that have the whole story thereof, true from the beginning even to the end.

A fragment of *Perlesvaus* dating from the fourteenth century is in the library of Wells Cathedral. A version of *Perlesvaus* appears in John of Glastonbury's *Chronicle*, so clearly Glastonbury possessed at that time a copy of this romance, which, as the author of Perlesvaus indicates, takes place around Glastonbury. It is here that the legends of Joseph of Arimathea and King Arthur become entwined, something Joseph Armitage Robinson found when he wrote his book, *Two Glastonbury Legends: King Arthur and Saint Joseph of Arimathea.*

Glastonbury not only became the center of Joseph's mission to Britain. It also stands at the head of the "Moors Adventurous": the sedge moors of Somerset where the Arthurian romances take place. Indeed, the stories of Arthur and the Grail are all imprinted in the landscape. The "right perilous and right adventurous" Black Chapel can be identified with the centuries-old chapel that once stood at Beckery to the southwest of Glastonbury. The mysterious Grail castle could have been at Ponters Ball, an iron-age earthwork to the east of Glastonbury, or it might have been Cadbury hill fort, believed by some to be the fabled Camelot. Pomparlès Bridge, once a stone bridge with four arches, where today the road crosses the river Brue between Street and Glastonbury, becomes the "Bridge Perilous." It was at this bridge, as John Leland, the king's antiquary, wrote during a visit in 1542, "men fable that Arture cast in his swerd," where, as his last act, Arthur returned his famous sword to the waters. Finally, from out of these Grail romances, Glastonbury is revealed to be Avalon.

An instance similar to the story in *Perlesvaus* of the miraculous power of the Grail to feed when in extreme need comes from the apocryphal *Vindicta Salvatoris*. This manuscript recounts how, when he was imprisoned for a period of forty years until he was released by the Roman emperor Vespasian, Joseph of Arimathea was fed daily by the Grail during his long imprisonment. This story had the effect of further substantiating the powers of the Grail, in this case as the means of Joseph's sustenance; and through this story, its association with the Last Supper and Joseph having used the cup to catch Jesus's blood from the cross, the Grail gradually came to be referred to as the Holy Grail.

However, notwithstanding the importance the Church placed on the story of Joseph's mission to Britain, it never accepted the story of the Grail, perhaps because the Church was vaguely aware of some pagan origins of the Grail similar to those Jessie Weston postulated in her book. As a consequence, depictions of Joseph of Arimathea in stained glass windows and other iconography show him holding, not a cup, but the two flasks or cruets in which it was said he had collected the blood and sweat of the Saviour. At Frecamp in Brittany there is a legend of a fig-tree log, washed miraculously ashore. It contained the cruets holding the blood and sweat of the crucified, having been set afloat, not by Joseph, but by his colleague, Nicodemus, in Palestine.

But as Frederick Bligh Bond points out in his book, *The Company of Avalon*, perhaps we have concentrated too much on thinking of the Grail as an actual vessel, whether it be a cup, a chalice, or even Joseph's two cruets, and we have forgotten that it is in reality an ideal to be rediscovered:

> That Ideal remains for us to rediscover, and we are to find it once again when we have risen above the danger which has all along attended man's use of symbol—the recurring danger of mistaking the symbol for that of which it is but the partial and imperfect image. . . . When we are free at last of this recurrent weakness, we become heirs of the Mystery of the Truth which all symbol is contrived to typify and express. The central Mystery is that which has been preserved in poetic imagery as the Holy Grail. Glaston was the guardian of it. Its symbol is the Cup, or Chalice, and men have been prone, in their ignorance and folly, to idolise the actual vessel, which was never more than the symbol of a deep truth living at the heart of Faith.

Bligh Bond believed that those who seek for the Grail Chalice in some secret hiding place in Glastonbury miss the point that the devotional ideal which the Grail expresses was translated into the architectural form that is Glastonbury Abbey, intuitively rendered in terms of the architectural symmetry and beauty embodied in the Old Church and the stones of the great abbey that grew up alongside it.

THE CHALICE WELL

The Chalice Well is a spring that flows out from the ground at the foot of Glastonbury Tor. When rain falls upon the Tor, the water that does not run off soaks into the ground where, passing through sandstone and limestone deposits, it emerges at a spring at the base of the Tor known as the White Spring. The remaining water percolates much deeper beneath the Tor where, passing through iron-rich deposits, it emerges as a reddened spring impregnated with iron at the Chalice Well or, to give it its other name, the Blood Well. The water runs down through the Chalice Well gardens, which are today owned and managed by a trust, founded by Wellesley Tudor Pole in 1959.

Legend attributes these two springs, the Blood or Chalice Well and the White Spring to Joseph of Arimathea having buried the two cruets containing the blood and sweat of Jesus's wounds below the adjacent Chalice Hill. Another legend says that Joseph buried the Grail cup or chalice close to the hill, hence the names Chalice Hill and Chalice Well.

The Chalice Well is said to be the oldest continuously used Holy Well in Britain, whose flow of 25,000 gallons a day in winter and 19,000 gallons in summer has never been known to fail. In the dry years of 1921–1922 it was the sole water supply available and saved the town of Glastonbury from drought. T.S. Eliot acknowledged Jessie Weston's book on the Grail, *From Ritual to Romance*, as crucial to understanding his poem, "The Waste Land." The suggestion that Joseph of Arimathea's buried Grail Chalice has saved Glastonbury from drought by supplying an unceasing flow of life-sustaining water provides us with a nice Christian parable of the Grail restoring to fecundity and life what would otherwise be a waste land.

FIVE

THE END OF JOSEPH'S LIFE

Finally, we have to consider where Joseph is buried. During the fifteenth century there were writers who held the view that he was buried in the precincts of Glastonbury Abbey, although no one could point to his grave. William Good, who as a boy had served in the chapel dedicated to Saint Joseph of Arimathea, said after the dissolution of the abbey that even the monks of Glastonbury Abbey had not known for certain where Joseph was buried. He said that the monks had been of the opinion that Joseph's body had been hidden, either in the abbey grounds, or on Ham Hill near Montacute. A cross known as the Holy Cross of Waltham was discovered on Ham Hill in around 1035. It is said that Canute's standard-bearer, Tovi, found the buried cross here, which was taken to Waltham, where at Tovi's shrine miraculous cures were said to have taken place. King Harold was cured of paralysis and a blind eye by the holy relic, and gratefully enlarged the shrine into Waltham Abbey. It is not possible to say with any certainty that Joseph would have left a cross on the hill before he went on to Glastonbury, but its discovery might be a sign that Joseph is buried there on the hill. William Good's account says that when Joseph's body is found, "the whole world will visit his grave on account of the many and wonderful miracles that will be worked there."

The sixteenth century metrical poem *The Lyfe of Joseph of Armathia*, says that Joseph was buried close to the old wattle oratory or church at Glastonbury:

> . . . and there they dyed; and Joseph was buryed nygh to the sayd oratory.

John of Glastonbury's *Chronicle of Glastonbury* includes a prophecy by the Welsh bard, Maelgwn of Llandaff, which dates from around 540. Maelgwn, also known as Melkin, reputedly instituted a bardic chair at Caerleon, and in the *Chronicle of Glastonbury* is spoken of as being "before Merlin." This strange piece of semi-poetical Latin prose which, according to Armitage Robinson, "is hardly capable of translation into English," thus becomes the earliest written account that we have of Joseph of Arimathea being in Britain.

Like *The Lyfe of Joseph of Armathia*, Maelgwn also locates Joseph's grave as being close to a wattle oratory, next to the southern corner of that oratory. The poem does not however mention Glastonbury; only that the grave is in the island of Avalon. It is clearly a huge cemetery, for the poem speaks of "countless thousands" of pagans entombed in the same ground as Joseph. There is the mystery of who is Abbadarè, described as "mighty in Saphat, noblest of pagans" who is apparently buried along with the thousands. The phrase, "the Prophet Jesus," is also unusual; no Christian writer would use such a phrase, which gives rise to the suggestion by some commentators that the poem is Eastern in origin. In some respects, Maelgwn's mention of Abbadarè and his description of the thousands entombed in Avalon being "more than all in the world beside, for the entombment of them all" seem to speak of a Celtic Otherworld or Paradise, rather than a particular location or place. This curious piece of Latin is given here, followed by the translation of Maelgwn's poem by Joseph Armitage Robinson:

> Insula Avallonis avida funere paganorum,præ ceteris in orbe ad seputuram eorum omnium sperulis prophe-ciæ vaticinantibus decorata, et in futurum ornata erit altissimum laudantibus. *Abbadare*, potens in *Saphat*, paganorum nobilissimus, cum centum quatuor milibus dormicionem ibi accepit. Inter quos Joseph de marmore, ab Arimathia nomine, cepit sompnum perpetuum; et jacet in linea bifurcata, juxta meridianum angulum oratorii, cratibus præparatis [*lge* ti], super potentem adorandam virginem, supradictis sperulatis locum habitantibus tredecim. Habet enim secum Joseph in sarcophago duo fassula alba et argentea, cruore prophetæ Ihesu et sudore perimpleta. Cum reperietur ejus sarcophagum integrum illibatum, in futuris videbitur, et erit apertum toto orbi terrarum. Extunc nec aqua, nec ros cœli, insulam nobilissimam

habitantibus poterit deficere. Per multum tempus ante diem judicialem in Iosaphat erunt aperta hæc, et viventibus declarata.

Here is the translation of Maelgwn's poem, which Armitage Robinson accompanies with an apology for having had to guess at the meaning of some of the words:

Avalon's island, with avidity
Claiming the death of pagans,
More than all in the world beside,
For the entombment of them all,
Honoured by chanting spheres of prophecy:
And for all time to come
Adornèd shall it be
By them that praise the Highest.
Abbadarè, mighty in Saphat,
Noblest of pagans,
With countless thousands
There hath fallen on sleep.
Amid these Joseph *de marmore*,
Of Arimathea by name,
Hath found perpetual sleep:
And he lies *in linea bifurcate*
Next the south corner of an oratory
Fashioned of wattles
For the adorning of a mighty Virgin
By the aforesaid sphere-betokened
Dwellers in that place, thirteen in all.
For Joseph hath with him

In his sarcophagus
Two cruets, white and silver,
Filled with the blood and sweat
Of the Prophet Jesus.
When his sarcophagus
Shall be found entire, intact,
In time to come, it shall be seen
And shall be open unto all the world:
Thenceforth nor water nor the dew of heaven
Shall fail the dwellers in that ancient isle.
For a long while before
The day of judgement in Josaphat
Open shall these things be
And declared to living men.

I have left two phrases in Armitage Robinson's English version of Maelgwn's poem untranslated, since in each case the Latin is capable of more than one meaning. The first phrase, *de marmore*, can be translated as "in marble," thought by some commentators to refer to Joseph's sarcophagus having been made from marble. But *de marmore* can also be translated as "of the sea"; this, I suggest, is the correct translation, and that it was written to identify that Joseph came from overseas for the benefit of readers who would not know where Arimathea was.

The translation of the second Latin phrase, *in linea bifurcata*, is of the greatest importance. It can be translated as "on a bifurcated line," which would make its object the indication of where in relation to the wattle oratory Joseph is buried. If we imagine the central body of the oratory as the nave of a ship—"nave" being the word we use today to describe the central area in a church—then the line in the poem, *in linea bifurcata, juxta meridianum angulum oratorii*, places Joseph's grave in what might be described as the helmsman's position in the nave of the oratory: the place where, if we were in a ship, in past times the ship would have been steered by use of a large oar fitted on the starboard side.

But *in linea bifurcata* can also refer to a shirt. A *linea* was a close-fitting undergarment, usually made of linen, while the epithet *bifurcata* implies that it had slits at the sides. So *in linea bifurcata* may be telling us that Joseph was buried next to the oratory in his shirt. We may recall that the Gospel as recorded by Saint Mark says that Joseph was instrumental in taking Jesus's body down from the cross. The metrical poem, *The Lyfe of Joseph of Armathia*, thought to have been written around 1502 and edited and printed by Walter Skeat in 1871, imagines that there was blood on Jesus's body and on the linen shroud in which Jesus was wrapped, and that some of this blood wiped off onto Joseph's shirt:

> But yet whan Ioseph Ihesu downe toke,
> The syd that the wound was on lay to his breast;
> The colde blode that was at our lordes herte rote
> Fell within Iosephes sherte and lay on his chest;
> Truly as holy scripture sayth there did it rest
> As the holy place aboue his stomake,

It would have been natural for Joseph to value this shirt, if it was bloodstained with Jesus's blood, as being precious to him, and if so it is quite conceivable that

Joseph chose to be buried in this garment. It would have been for Joseph a memento of the day when he took the body of Jesus down from the cross and buried it in the tomb that he had cut out of the rock: the tomb that was to have been the eventual resting place for his own body, but which was now far away in the garden of a property in Jerusalem that Joseph had once owned.

AVALON

Maelgwn of Llandaff's poem says that it is in "Avalon's island" that Joseph of Arimathea "hath found perpetual sleep." Enter Glastonbury today or purchase a map of the area, and you will soon be told that here is Avalon. Avalon is not only connected to Joseph: it is most famously the fabled place to which, according to Geoffrey of Monmouth in his *History of the Kings of Britain* written around 1138, the mortally wounded King Arthur was ferried on a ghostly ship following the battle of Camlan against his nephew, Mordred, who had usurped Arthur's throne while Arthur was away from home:

> It was there that we took Arthur after the battle of Camlan where he had been wounded, Barin was the steersman because of his knowledge of the seas and the stars of heaven. With him at the tiller of the ship, we arrived there with the prince; and Morgen received us with due honour. She put the king in her chamber on a golden bed, uncovered his wound with her noble hand and looked long at it. At length she said he could be cured if only he stayed with her a long while and accepted her treatment. We therefore happily committed the king to her care and spread our sails to favourable winds on our return journey.

A very similar account appears in the *Life of Merlin*, a Latin poem of Geoffrey's time and claiming to be written by Geoffrey himself. In it, the bard Taliesson is made to describe the voyage that the wounded Arthur embarked at much greater length. The island to which he is taken is not actually called by the name of Avalon, but is:

> The Isle of Apples, called the Fortunate Isle. Here, there is no tilling of the soil: nature unassisted brings forth her corn and fruits: life is extended to a hundred years or more. Nine sisters gently rule this Happy Land. The eldest, Morgen, is the fairest and the most skilled. She knows how to change her shape and fly like Daedalus whither she may desire. In medicine, too, she is supreme. To her the king is brought, and she probes his wound, and at last declares that he will recover, if he will abide a long time under her care.

The lady Morgen (sometimes spelled Muirgein) referred to was Arthur's half-sister. The account in Geoffrey of Monmouth's *History of the Kings of Britain* appears to be describing a journey to Avalon by sea, rather than overland through the marshes to Glastonbury. Geoffrey of Monmouth makes a further connection of Arthur with Avalon when he states in his *History* that Arthur's sword, Caliburn (i.e., Excalibur) was forged "in the fabled isle of Avalon." The fourteenth century English poem, *Libeaus Desconnus* tells how, under instructions from the dying Arthur, his sword was cast into the waters that flow beneath the bridge, Pomparles—the Arthurian *Bridge Perilous*, that today crosses the river Brue on the road between Glastonbury and Street.

The French romance *Perlesvaus* describes Avalon as a place where holy hermits, each living in their separate cell, worshipped together in a chapel. Whether or not Glastonbury is being described here, and there are certain features in this account that appear to correspond with Glastonbury, this is how as a holy settlement it would have looked before it later developed into a monastery with monks and its first Saxon abbot, Beorhtwald, in the latter part of the seventh century:

> He [Lancelot] looketh to the right, and on the top of the mountain beside the valley he seeth a chapel newly builded. . . . By the side of this chapel were three houses dight [decorated] right richly, each standing by itself facing the chapel. There was a right fair graveyard round about the chapel, that was enclosed at the compass of the forest, and a spring came down. . . . And each of the houses had its own orchard, and the orchard an enclosure. Lancelot heareth vespers being chanted in the chapel. . . . There were three hermits therewithin that had sung their vespers. . . . And they told him that the place there was Avalon.

If Joseph of Arimathea was buried in Avalon, the question of when Glastonbury became equated with Avalon is important to this biography of Joseph's life. Indeed, there is a greater question: what or where is Avalon? Is it found at Glastonbury? Was it even a known locality, or was it perhaps a name for the Celtic Paradise?

It appears that the earliest record on the identification of Avalon with Glastonbury comes from Giraldus Cambrensis—Gerald of Wales, to give him his anglicized name. In his book, *De Principis Instructione*, written around 1194, Giraldus speaks of King Arthur as having had a special devotion to Saint Mary of Glastonbury, and that he had been a patron of the Old Church. Giraldus tells of the discovery 'in our times' of the tomb of Arthur and Guenevere at Glastonbury, and he later writes, "what is now called 'Glastonia' was anciently called 'insula Avalonia.'"

We have no grounds for supposing that Geoffrey of Monmouth identified the isle of Avalon with Glastonbury, for when he speaks of Avalon he describes it as "The island of Apples":

> The island of Apples, which men call the Fortunate Isle, is so named because it produces all things of itself. The fields there have no need of farmers to plough them, and Nature alone provides all cultivation. Grain and grapes are produced without tending, and apple trees grow in the woods from close-clipped grass. The earth of its own accord brings forth not merely grass but all things in superabundance.

Geoffrey's description of Avalon has prompted etymologists—though not all agree—to postulate that the word Avalon derives from the Welsh *affalen*, an "apple tree." Certainly the county of Somerset, if not specifically Glastonbury, is well known for its cider apples. But apples are grown in many other places, yet not all are designated as Avalon. But there is another kind of apple that the medieval abbey at Glastonbury would have prized more highly than edible apples.

These are the apples that form on oak trees around the eggs laid by female gall wasps. The Welsh word for an "apple"—afal—is also the word for an oak apple or gall. We know that the oak was reverenced by the Druids. To the northeast of Glastonbury Tor there is an ancient Druidic grove of oak trees, the remnants of giant oaks that once grew there, two of which were known locally as Gog and Magog, and on which oak apples probably appeared at different times. The importance of oak apples was that, when crushed, they yielded gallotannic acid, which when added to ferrous sulphate with something like gum arabic to bind the whole together, created a long lasting purple-black ink. This was highly sought after by religious houses for writing on vellum, and without it we would not have such beautiful works today as the Book of Kells or the Lindisfarne Gospels. Even Columba, who was forced into exile on account of his copying in his own hand a rare and valuable Psalter, praised the "heaven's angels that come and go under every leaf" of the oaks that grew in his beloved Derry. Columba's "heaven's angels" are clearly the female gall wasps from which the oak apples provided him with the valued ink.

Geoffrey of Monmouth says that the Isle of Avalon is also known as "the Fortunate Isle." There are other places named "the Fortunate Isles," or "the Isles of the Blessed." The Scilly Islands, lying off the southwest coast of Britain, are known by some as the Hesperides—the "Blessed Isles." As the Cassiterides, the ancient name for the tin bearing islands, they have a close connection with Joseph of Arimathea who in our tradition was a trader in tin. Even the description in *The High History of the Holy Graal* of Avalon being a place where there were holy hermits, each living in separate cells, corresponds closely to the Greek geographer Strabo's account of tin traders and a brotherhood living on the Scillys:

> The Cassiterides are ten in number and lie near each other in the ocean towards the north from the haven of the Artabri (Corunna). One of them is desert, but the others are inhabited by men in black cloaks, clad in tunics reaching to the feet, girt about the breast, and walking with staves, thus resembling the furies we see in tragic representations . . . Of the metals they have tin and lead which, with skins, they barter with the merchants for earthenware, salt and brazen metals.

Plutarch, a Greek historian and Roman citizen from the first and second centuries AD who wrote a life of Quintus Sertorius, a Roman statesman who lived around 100 BC, quotes what Sertorius had learnt from Spanish sailors:

> The islands are said to be two in number, separated by a very narrow strait, and lie 10,000 furlongs [roughly, 1,250 miles] from Africa. They are called the Isles of the Blessed.

Plutarch adds that the islands "abound in fruit and birds of every kind," and were but a few days' sea-journey from Spain. The difference in the number of islands quoted by Strabo and Plutarch can be explained by the fact that, over time, differences in sea levels have changed the number of islands visible in the Scillies. So even the Scilly Islands can lay claim to being Avalon: the place where the ship bearing the mortally wounded Arthur sailed following his defeat at the battle of Camlan, which some writers place in Cornwall. It also opens up a possibility that Joseph, through his connection to the trade in tin, could be buried on the Scilly Islands.

MARY

Earlier, I wrote of the possibility of Mary, the mother of Jesus, having accompanied Joseph of Arimathea as he left France for Britain. If Mary did accompany Joseph and remained with him for the rest of her life, then she too must be buried in Britain. Mary is known by various names: "Our Lady," the "Virgin Mary," or more simply, the "Virgin." It is this last name, describing her as "mighty," that appears in Armitage Robinson's English version of Maelgwn of Llandaff's poem, where it says:

> . . . Amid these Joseph *de marmore*,
> Of Arimathea by name,
> Hath found perpetual sleep:
> And he lies *in linea bifurcata*
> Next the south corner of an oratory
> Fashioned of wattles
> For the adorning of a mighty Virgin

However, if we examine the original Latin of the poem we find that the line translated 'For the adorning of a mighty Virgin' has omitted one important word—"super." The actual Latin reads: *super potentam adorandum virginem*, where the word "super" means "over" or "above." Thus, a more accurate translation would read that Joseph lies in his grave "*over* the powerful adorable Virgin." Such a translation points to Joseph of Arimathea and Mary the mother of Jesus being buried together. Curious, too, is the reference to the Virgin Mary as "mighty." Although Mary succeeded to many titles, "mighty" was not one of them. She did indeed in time become Queen of Heaven, but she is always seen to remain lowly and accessible to the faithful.

Maelgwn of Llandaff's prophetic poem says that there were 'Dwellers in that place, thirteen in all.' which reveals there had been an additional person living with Joseph and his eleven companions. We may also recall that we read earlier how, digging deep in the area occupied by the earliest cemetery which he had carefully identified as lying south of the post-1184 Lady Chapel at Glastonbury Abbey, the archaeologist Dr. Raleigh Radford discovered two low rectangular tombs, each large enough to hold two bodies, that appeared to have been for persons of special importance. Could one of these have been Joseph's and Mary's grave?

Set into the southern wall of the ruined Lady Chapel that stands on the site where the old wattle church stood prior to the abbey being built at Glastonbury, there is a stone with the words "Jesus Maria" carved on it. William Good, who as we learnt earlier had served in the chapel dedicated to Saint Joseph of Arimathea, and who had later witnessed the dissolution of the abbey, remarks on this stone with its 'characters of great age' carved on it. Even today, among those who care for Glastonbury Abbey there is uncertainty and a range of different opinions regarding the meaning of this stone. Perhaps it is another link of the Virgin Mary with these shores. Perhaps, too, it is a pointer to the truth of the tradition that Jesus built the original wattle oratory that became the Old Church. It certainly faces that part of the cemetery where Dr. Raleigh Radford discovered the tombs constructed to hold two bodies. Whatever its origin and history, one cannot but feel that this stone with its inscription "Jesus Maria" marks some hallowed spot close to the chapel dedicated to Our Lady and where, in the crypt below, Saint Joseph of Arimathea was once venerated.

JOSEPH'S GRAVE

With the growing importance of his cult to Glastonbury Abbey, the need to establish where Joseph of Arimathea was buried became a pressing one. So in 1345, King Edward III issued a royal writ and a license to John Bloome of London to dig in the grounds of Glastonbury Abbey in the search for Joseph's grave, provided the Abbot and monks permitted it:

> The King to all to whom these presents shall come, greeting. John Bloome of London has petitioned us that since (as he asserts) a divine injunction has been laid on him as concerning the venerable body of the noble decurion Joseph of Arimathea, which rests in Christ buried within the bounds of the monastery of Glastonbury, and is to be revealed in these days to the honour and the edification of many; to wit, that he should seek it diligently until he find it; because it is said to be contained in certain ancient writings that his body was there buried: We therefore (if it so be) desiring to pay devout honour to his sepulchre and to the relics of him who performed such offices of religion and humanity to our Redeemer in His death, taking down His body from the cross and laying it in his own new sepulchre; and hoping for ourselves and all our realm a wealth of grace from the revelation aforesaid; Have conceded and licence given, so far as rests with us, to the said John that he should have the power to

> dig within the precinct of the said monastery and seek for those precious relics according to the injunction and the revelation made to him in the places where he shall see it to be most suitable: Provided however that this can be done without hurt to our beloved in Christ the abbot and convent of the said monastery and without destruction of their church and houses there; and that for this purpose he have the licence and assent of the abbot and convent themselves.
>
> In testimony whereof, &c. Witness the King at Westminster, on the tenth day of June. By the King himself.

The only evidence that the abbot and convent gave their permission for the search, or whether the search was successful or fruitless, comes from an anonymous East Anglian chronicler, who has this brief entry under the year, 1367: "The bodies of Joseph of Arimathea and his companions were found at Glastonbury." If the grave of Joseph of Arimathea had been found at Glastonbury we may be certain that the abbey would have publicized it widely and capitalized on it as far as attracting pilgrims and their monies was concerned. If his grave had been opened and the two cruets containing Jesus's blood and sweat found inside, these would have been the greatest relics in all of Christendom and people would have flocked from all over the world to view them. Since there is no record of any of the above having taken place, we may take it that, whether he was permitted by the abbot and the monks to dig in the abbey precincts or not, Joseph's grave was not discovered by John Bloom.

Later, around or shortly after 1500, the abbot of Glastonbury, Abbot Beere, established a chapel and shrine to Saint Joseph in a crypt that he had dug beneath the Lady Chapel in the abbey. In doing so, the abbot caused all the earth that had once been the floor of the wattle oratory called the Old Church to be removed and deposited elsewhere. If the grave of Joseph, or indeed any grave that had been beneath the old wattle oratory had been found, Abbot Beere would have made a great deal of such a find. But he did not, so we must conclude that no graves were discovered when the crypt for the Saint Joseph Chapel was excavated.

M. A. Kelly in his *Maelgwn of Llandaff and Joseph of Arimathea* writes that he believes the grave of Joseph to be in the grounds of Cardiff Castle. Kelly says that when Maelgwn was writing his poem describing burials in the Isle of Avalon, including that of Joseph of Arimathea, it is far more likely that he was writing of somewhere in the vicinity of south Wales where Maelgwn lived as a bard, rather than writing of Glastonbury which is many miles away. I wrote earlier that the land known as south Wales once extended down to the river Parret in Somerset, and therefore close to Glastonbury. Nevertheless, M.A. Kelly believes that the Isle of Avalon was formed when the river Taff split in two south of Llandaff Cathedral and rejoined south of Cardiff Castle. An old ruined Chapel of St. Mary stands in the grounds of Cardiff Castle, where once stood a monastery of the Black Friars. It is here that Kelly believes the grave of Joseph of Arimathea is still to be seen today, lying, as one translation of Maelgwn's poem reads, "in the southern angle of the bifurcated line" of the old chapel's foundations in the ruined Black Friars monastery at Bute Park.

The Rev. Lionel Smithett Lewis, writing in his *St. Joseph of Arimathea at Glastonbury*, believes that Joseph's grave was actually discovered in Glastonbury Abbey as a result of John Bloom's excavations, and that Joseph's remains were placed in a large altar tomb that stood at the east end of Abbot Beere's crypt dedicated to Saint Joseph. Smithett Lewis writes that it was Ralph de Coggeshall in a Lincolnshire monastery who was the "anonymous East Anglian chronicler" who reported in 1367 that "The bodies of Joseph of Arimathea and his companions were found at Glastonbury." No mention is made of cruets containing the blood and sweat of Jesus being found in Joseph's grave. Smithett Lewis writes that Joseph's remains were placed in a silver casket, which was then deposited in the altar tomb in the crypt. In 1662 this altar tomb was hastily removed by night from the ruined crypt and placed in the churchyard of the Church of Saint John in Glastonbury. In 1928 it was brought into the church and placed in the chapel dedicated to Saint Catherine in the north transept of the church, where it stands today. It is certainly a very ancient altar tomb, with a caduceus carved at one end of the tomb. But is it the tomb of Joseph of Arimathea, who gave up the tomb that he had originally carved out of the rock for himself in his garden in Jerusalem and gave it to Christ?

We may never discover the answer to this question, and perhaps we do not need to. I began this book by saying that no one today knows for certain where Arimathea, the birthplace of Joseph, was. Now we have discovered that no one knows for certain where Joseph is buried. But between his birth and his death, what I hope this book has revealed and brought out of obscurity is the life of this great man who braved everything and gambled his home, his wealth, and his position in Judean society to give the body of Jesus a decent burial, and who later, thanks to his continued courage, brought the life and story of the risen Christ to Britain. I hope that you, the reader, agree with me that we owe Joseph of Arimathea a great debt of gratitude.

BIBLIOGRAPHY

All Bible references are taken from The Holy Bible in Modern English in the translation by Ferrar Fenton, published by Destiny Publishers, Merrimac, Massachusetts, U.S.A., unless otherwise stated.

Armitage Robinson, J.	*Two Glastonbury Legends*. Cambridge University Press, 1926.
Bligh Bond, Frederick.	*The Gate of Remembrance*. Thorsons Publishers, 1978.
________.	*The Company of Avalon*. Basil Blackwell, 1924.
Carley, James P.	*Glastonbury Abbey: The Holy House at the Head of the Moors Adventurous*. Gothic Image Publications, 1988.
Jenkins, Elizabeth.	*The Mystery of King Arthur*. Michael O'Mara Books, 1990.
Kelly, M. A.	*Maelgwn of Llandaff and Joseph of Arimathea*. Ed. Michael A. Clark. The Covenant Publishing Co., 2013.
Lewis, Glyn S.	*Did Jesus Come to Britain?* Clairview Books, 2008.
Lewis, Lionel S.	*St. Joseph of Arimathea at Glastonbury*. The Lutterworth Press, 1988.
Strachan, Gordon.	*Jesus the Master Builder*. Floris Books, 2001.
Weston, Jessie L.	*From Ritual to Romance: The Search for the Grail*. Republished Classics, 2013.
Editors: various.	*The Somerset Wetlands*. Somerset Books, 2008.

INDEX